1/21

THE EIGHTY-DOLLAR
CHAMPION

BOOKS BY ELIZABETH LETTS

The Perfect Horse

The Eighty-Dollar Champion

THE EIGHTY-DOLLAR CHAMPION

THE TRUE STORY OF A HORSE, A MAN, AND AN UNSTOPPABLE DREAM

ELIZABETH LETTS

DELACORTE PRESS

Visit us on the Web! rhcbooks.com

Educators and librarians, for a variety of teaching tools, visit us at
RHTeachersLibrarians.com

Library of Congress Cataloging-in-Publication Data
Names: Letts, Elizabeth, author.
Title: The eighty-dollar champion : a man, a horse, and an unstoppable dream / Elizabeth Letts.
Description: New York : Delacorte Press, [2020] | Based on the nonfiction book of the same
title originally published: New York : Ballantine Books, 2011. | Includes bibliographical
references and index. | Audience: Ages 8–12. | Audience: Grades 4–6. | Summary: In 1958,
a horse bound for the slaughterhouse is purchased by a man who names him Snowman and
takes him to the top of equestrian show jumping.
Identifiers: LCCN 2019043390 (print) | LCCN 2019043391 (ebook) |
ISBN 978-0-593-12712-4 (hardcover) | ISBN 978-0-593-12714-8 (ebook) |
ISBN 978-0-593-12713-1 (lib. bdg.)
Subjects: LCSH: Snowman, 1949–1974—Juvenile fiction. | CYAC: Snowman, 1949–1974—
Fiction. | Show jumping—Fiction. | Horses—Fiction.
Classification: LCC PZ10.3.L5534 Eig 2020 (print) | LCC PZ10.3.L5534 (ebook) |
DDC [Fic]—dc23

The text of this book is set in 12-point Adobe Jenson Pro.
Interior design by Ken Crossland

Printed in the United States of America
10 9 8 7 6 5 4 3 2 1
First Edition

This book is dedicated to Harry and his family
and to the memory of the gallant horse
Snowman

So many of our dreams at first seem impossible, then they seem improbable, and then, when we summon the will, they soon become inevitable.

—CHRISTOPHER REEVE

CONTENTS

THE EIGHTY-DOLLAR
CHAMPION

CHAPTER 1

THE LAST HORSES

NEW HOLLAND, PENNSYLVANIA, 1956

One Monday morning in February 1956, a big gray horse stood quietly in a small wooden pen, waiting patiently for his turn. He wore only a rough rope halter. A number was pasted on his bony hip. His coat was marred with dirt and his mane needed a trim. But despite his condition, he had a kindly look in his big brown eyes. In a minute, it would be his turn to trot across the auction ring. People who had come to the sale to purchase a horse would look him over, and with luck, someone would offer to buy him. If this happened, he'd leave this rough wooden enclosure for good and head to a new home. But this large gentle creature with the soft look in his eyes had clearly been neglected and did not look his best. Would anyone choose him? Or would he soon return to his paddock, unwanted?

A handler jerked the big gray's lead rope, and the animal perked up, as if he wanted to put on his best show. In spite of the handler's rough movements, the gray followed willingly, trotting briskly across the sales arena, his head held proudly high, his ears pricked forward, his ragged and tangled tail appearing almost to float behind him. His eager manner seemed to say, "Look at me!" But the people watching the horse as he passed hardly seemed to care. Some glanced briefly and looked away, while others frowned. Did they see only his dirty coat and missing shoe? Did no one notice the proud look in his eyes?

Once, twice, three times, the man jogged the gray across the arena. But not a single person raised a hand to signal they were interested in buying him. After the third turn, the handler shrugged, dropped to a walk, and headed the horse toward the exit as the auctioneer called out, "*Next!*" The gentle gray's head seemed to droop a bit as he returned to his rough pen. What would happen to him next?

On that same Monday in February 1956, a horseback riding teacher named Harry de Leyer was running late. The headlights didn't work on his beat-up old station wagon. A new car would have been far more than the Dutch immigrant could afford. And now, although he had woken long before dawn on this wintry morning, the snow and a flat tire had set him back. He was headed toward the small town of New Holland, Pennsylvania, where one of the biggest horse auctions in America was held every Monday. He had driven hours from his home in New York, hoping to buy a quiet lesson horse for his riding pupils at the Knox School on Long Island, New York. But he was behind schedule because of the snowstorm and was worried that by the time he got there, all the good horses would have already been sold.

Harry didn't have much money to spend. He had brought along just eighty dollars, all he could spare, which wasn't much for a horse. Fancy horses cost hundreds, even thousands of dollars, but Harry knew that the auction might be a good place to find a cheap one. Some of the animals at the auction would be too old, too feeble, too lame to make good riding horses. Still, Harry knew that sometimes there were decent mounts to be found—sturdy, kind, quiet horses. Horses who just needed another chance. Maybe, just maybe, eighty dollars would be enough.

The stables on the auction grounds were not fancy—just simple wooden structures to hold the horses while they waited their turn to go up for sale. Every Monday, the pens would fill up with horses of all sizes, ages, and breeds—palominos and Percherons, trotters and Thoroughbreds.

The best horses were snatched up early; sometimes more than one person wanted the same horse, sparking a bidding war. Some were giant workhorses, strong enough to pull the heaviest plow; some were adorable ponies, just waiting for a child to love. But others were ordinary animals—maybe a little old, or tired, maybe a bit dirty, or down on their luck. Those horses needed good homes, too, but the good homes were sometimes hard to find.

Handlers led the horses one by one across a large arena while families leaned up against the railings to take a good look at each prospect. If you wanted to buy one, you had to raise your hand quick. You had only a minute or two to make up your mind. By the end of the auction, two to three hundred horses would have trotted across the arena. Most of them found a buyer and headed off to a new home, where they would be loved and treated kindly.

But every Monday, some horses were left behind. Big ones and small ones, dark ones and light ones. Horses too old, too thin, too sick, or sometimes just too plain to win a buyer's heart. They trotted across the big sales arena once, twice, three times, and prospective buyers looked them up and down, but no one raised a hand to buy. Sadly, the horses returned to their stalls, unwanted.

These leftover horses—these neglected creatures—wouldn't have another chance to find a loving home. There was a man who bought the extra horses, paying just a few dollars each. Then this man, the kill buyer, sold the last horses to the slaughterhouse.

It was getting so late that Harry was afraid he was going to miss the horse sale entirely. He drove down the snowy roads as fast as he dared, but when he finally arrived at the Amish Country auction, his heart sank. The grounds were deserted and the snowy parking lot was almost empty. Only one vehicle remained, a battered old truck with slatted sides. It looked more like a cattle car than a proper van. A bunch of horses, fifteen or so, were crowded in its back. A rough man dressed in a barn jacket and jeans was hurriedly closing the ramp.

Unwilling to give up after his long drive, Harry leaned out his car window and called out to him: "Are those horses for sale?"

"Nothing left but the kills," the man called back, without a glance Harry's way. He seemed as though he didn't want to be bothered, but Harry could see the horses inside the van. He wanted to take a closer look.

Getting out of his car, he walked over and peered into the

truck's gloomy interior. In a proper horse van, horses travel in padded stalls, their legs bandaged in thick cotton batting, with fresh hay suspended within reach. But this van offered nothing like that. More than a dozen horses were packed together on the bare metal floor, fenced in by rough slats that did nothing to protect them from the elements or from one another. Harry could smell fear rising from them; the sound of hooves striking metal was almost deafening, and in the shadowy interior he saw flashes of white in their eyes as the horses jostled up against each other. As if they knew there was trouble ahead for them.

As Harry watched, a pair of large brown eyes caught his attention. One of the horses was standing quietly, crammed up against the truck's side. This calm creature seemed to pay no mind to the chaos around him. Harry reached out his palm to the horse, and the animal stuck his nose toward him, blowing warm breath onto Harry's hand. Those brown eyes were still looking at him. Asking.

"What about that one?" Harry said.

The man was already all loaded up, ready to drive away. "You don't want that one. He's missing a shoe and his front is all cut up from pulling a harness."

"I just want to take a look," Harry said.

The man sighed. Grudgingly, he backed the brown-eyed horse out of the trailer. Scrambling down the steep ramp, the horse almost fell. He righted himself swiftly.

Once the animal was off the trailer, Harry got a better picture. It wasn't a pretty one.

The big horse was male, a gelding, as Harry had expected. His coat, the dull white color that horsemen call gray, was matted and caked with mud. Open wounds marred both knees. His hooves were grown out and cracked, and a shoe was missing. The horse was thin, but not completely undernourished—not as bad off as the horses normally seen in a kill van. The marks across his chest showed that he'd once pulled a heavy harness. He had a deep chest; Harry noticed the strong, well-muscled shoulders, probably developed by pulling a plow.

The horse's teeth showed that he was "aged"—not younger than eight years old, and quite possibly older. Harry scanned his legs, and found no obvious flaws. This horse had no ailments: he was just undernourished, beat-up, and broken-down. An ordinary horse who had hit hard times.

The man dropped the rope on the ground, but the horse made no move to run. He followed Harry with calm eyes. When Harry spoke a few words to him, he pricked his ears forward. They were small and well formed, curving inward at the tips.

Harry took a harder look at the horse underneath the caked-on dirt. Even cleaned up and well fed, this gelding would never be beautiful. He was as plain-faced and friendly as a favorite mutt—wide-eyed and eager to please. A man's-best-friend kind of horse.

The horse stretched his neck forward. Harry reached out, sorry that he had no carrot or sugar cube to offer. He had nothing to give but the palm of his hand.

Despite the gray's sorry condition, a spark of life lit up his brown eyes. He had a strong body that would fill out with proper care. Any horseman can recognize an animal whose spirit has been broken, from the listless head and dull eyes, the slack lips and shuffling gait. But this horse was not broken—he had an air of self-possession. All he needed was someone to care for him. Harry was sure that if he was given affection, this horse would return it in abundance.

But Harry knew he couldn't be that person. The de Leyers counted every penny. There was no room in his life for an old, skinny horse.

"You want him or not?" the driver asked impatiently.

Making it in the equestrian business meant being hard-hearted. You couldn't take a chance on just any horse, even if it was a charming and friendly one. For every animal that might become a riding horse, a dozen *other* horses were too old or too creaky-boned to even stand a chance. Common sense told Harry he should keep his cash in his pocket. His wife, Johanna, and their children would be waiting for him at home.

The slaughter truck yawned open behind them. The horses were scrambling against each other; a few more minutes and a fight might break out. One sign from Harry, and the truck driver would lead the big gray back up that ramp. The story would finish quickly. First, a cold, crowded, terrifying ride. Then the short, tragic end.

The thought made Harry flinch.

Harry knew what it felt like to be powerless. Before im-migrating to America, he had lived through World War II and the Nazi invasion. Back in Harry's village in Holland, the day the Nazi soldiers led the horses away, the villagers had stood with their hands clenched at their sides, trying to hide the tears in their eyes.

Yes, just like this horse, Harry had seen a lot in his young life. Beat-up or not, the horse seemed brave. Harry noted the quiet way he stood there, the look in his eyes that said he was ready to trust. Horses are herd animals. They smell fear, and sense danger. But this horse held out hope. He seemed to put his trust in Harry, even though it was clear that, so far, men had treated him poorly.

The horse stood motionless, square on all fours, holding Harry's steady gaze.

"How much you want for him?" Harry replied finally.

The man grinned broadly, probably thinking he stood a chance to make a buck on this guy. "You can have him for eighty."

Harry averted his eyes, fingering the rolled-up bills in his pocket. He could buy a lot of meals for his family for eighty dollars, a lot of bales of hay and sacks of grain for the horses he already had. It was hard to imagine facing his wife with his money spent and nothing but this broken-down ex–plow horse to show for it.

Hadn't Harry gotten over being a sucker for horses?

But there was something about this one. Harry turned back and the horse was still watching him intently. This gentle gelding was wise, an old soul, a horse whose eyes seemed to cover hidden depths.

Man or beast, Harry did not like to see a proud soul held in captivity.

"Might make a lesson horse, if we can fatten him up," Harry said.

He handed over the eighty dollars and never looked back.

CHAPTER 2

ON THE WAY HOME

ST. JAMES, LONG ISLAND, 1956

Eighty dollars poorer, Harry had made a deal. Now it was time to hit the long road home. The truck driver was heading back to New York anyway, he said, so he agreed to drop the eighty-dollar horse at Harry's barn. Nothing left for Harry but the long drive back through the snow in his beat-up Ford. Maybe he could make good time and get home to his family before nightfall.

As he drove, Harry pondered his purchase. A horse for sale is more than a flesh-and-blood animal. He is also a creature full of promise. Along with a horse's physical traits—coat color, four legs, a strong back, a friendly expression—he also carries hope: that he will be strong and brave, faithful and true.

And for anyone who works in the horse business, horses are also about making money—whether in horse shows for professionals, or in riding stables for beginners.

Harry had already discovered that the best way for a riding teacher to make money was to find a horse with potential, sell it, and make a profit. Easier said than done. Harry had no money. That was why he set his sights on reject horses, the ones that no one else wanted. Harry considered himself sensible when it came to picking out horses that would help his business, though he also had to admit that he seldom met a horse he did not like.

Leaving Pennsylvania, Harry navigated his way back home. On the road, the black carriages pulled by Amish teams reminded him of home in Europe. The simple farms and the horse-drawn wagons were just like the ones in St. Oedenrode, the village he had grown up in, before it had been ravaged by the Second World War.

The farther Harry got from Pennsylvania, though, the more the world around him changed and looked more modern. In a way, the highways Harry drove down mirrored his own journey, just six years earlier, from a small Dutch farm to America. When he and his wife had arrived from their village, Harry had little more than a strong back and a gift for horses. Now he lived only fifty miles from New York City, the biggest city on earth.

Big American cars, decked out with chrome and fins, zoomed along the new interstate. These days, more and more farmland was being turned into housing, suburban shopping centers, drive-in movies, supermarkets, and motels—all of which catered to the new driving lifestyle. The cars themselves looked futuristic almost, like rocket ships. Though money was very tight in America, it was clear that the age of the automobile was here to stay.

The country's economic troubles didn't affect Harry that much. He and Johanna had lived on a strict budget since the day they'd arrived in America. As Harry drove up the new freeway in his battered old car, what he saw around him was a land of opportunity.

After making his way through New York City, Harry started the long trek across Long Island, all the way to Suffolk County. Harry breathed easier as he left behind the noise and confusion of the city and suburbs. The gray waters of Long Island Sound faded into the patchy, sandy soil where farmers grew potatoes. St. James, where he was headed, was a peaceful town on Long Island's North Shore. The area around St. James was a summer retreat for rich New Yorkers, with its huge, wealthy estates. But there were also small farmers and tradesmen—and some hard-working immigrants like himself. It was a good place to raise a family.

Harry got home before the horse trailer arrived. It was snowing hard as he pulled into the driveway. The de Leyers' three-story farmhouse on Moriches Road was lit up and looked welcoming and warm. Harry's job as a riding instructor at the Knox School had brought the de Leyer family something they could have only dreamed of before: their own home. Sure, it was a converted chicken farm on a modest lot. But it was theirs.

Harry had single-handedly rebuilt the chicken coop into a stable for horses. It was too small for a *proper* horse establishment, but at least he had his own piece of ground. He'd proudly named it Hollandia Farms, after his homeland. As he turned off the ignition, the car shuddered to a stop. It felt good to have a place to call home. Soon, Johanna and the children would rush out the door to welcome him.

Just then, the truck driver from the auction pulled into the de Leyer driveway. The dilapidated truck looked like no place for a horse, especially on a frigid night like this. The weary, brown-eyed beast peered through the vehicle's slatted sides. He saw people come out into the cold to greet his arrival. Every sight, every smell, every sound must have been unfamiliar to him.

The whole family hurried outside at the sound of the truck arriving. Harry's three children were lined up in a row, bundled up in jackets and boots. And Johanna was carrying the youngest, Marty, in her arms. Everyone was eager to see the newest member of their family.

The grumpy driver untied the horse's rope and put the ramp down, then tugged on the horse's tail.

The big gray stumbled as he clambered down, then stood blinking in the light glowing from the house. Nobody said a word. Harry had already forgotten what a sorry state this animal was in—scrawny and underfed, covered with sores, his unkempt mane matted. Even at night, he could see the dark stains, the knocked-up knees and harness rubs. He wondered what the family would think about this sorry-looking horse.

But when the giant creature turned his head and caught Harry's eye, he felt it again—that sense of connection.

The children looked the horse over carefully, saying nothing.

The gray stood still, ears pricked forward, eager as a puppy wanting to be adopted from the pound. Snow drifted down, leaving a dusting across his broad haunches.

Harriet, age four, broke the silence and chimed:

"Look, Daddy, he has snow all over him. He looks just like a snowman."

Yes, the other children agreed, a snowman!

Stains marred the horse's coat, making it hard to imagine

that he would ever clean up, or look anything but dingy. But the children didn't care about those blemishes or the shaggy mane. They didn't notice the untended hooves or the missing shoe. To them, the horse was a white and gleaming wonder. A snowman. That soon became his official name.

It was a hopeful beginning.

The truck driver turned his big old truck around and rattled out of the de Leyer driveway. Snowman didn't even look back. As Harry grasped the lead rope, the horse followed along quietly, as though he knew he was home. He went calmly into a stall and started munching on hay without so much as a skittish look around. Harry had given him one of the box stalls, knowing the horse needed to move and stretch his legs after the long, hard ride in the crowded truck. Now he filled the stall with straw, even adding a little extra to make the bed soft.

Before Harry went back into the house, he slipped off his wooden shoes, leaving them by the door, then turned to look back at the quiet stable. Yes, he thought, this horse would clean up just fine.

In the de Leyer household, everyone did everything together. That meant that a new horse in the barn was a project for the whole family. Their first order of business was to nurse Snowman back to health.

Harry pulled his mane, trimmed his whiskers, and replaced his missing shoe. Joseph, whose nickname was Chef, and Harriet were assigned the job of currying him—using a hard comb to bring up dander so that his coat underneath started to shine.

It took several sudsings from top to toe to get him clean. The coat that emerged from under the filth was the color horsemen call "flea-bitten" gray: white with small brown flecks.

The gray stood quiet for grooming. His manners were very polite, as if he knew he had come to a place where he would be cared for. He was good-sized, with the strong muscles of a workhorse, and, though thin, he was not completely wasted. With a new diet of fresh hay and plump oats, he filled out quickly. Flesh padded his ribs and covered his bony hips. He'd never win a beauty contest, but after a short time in the de Leyer barn, Snowman lost that neglected look. He started to resemble an animal who was loved.

After a few days of rest and food for Snowman, Harry decided it was time to see what the big horse could do. He slipped an old bridle over Snowman's ears and slipped a bit into his mouth. The bit, a rubber D-ring snaffle, was soft and comfortable on the horse's mouth.

The whole family gathered to watch as Snowman started his first training lesson. Harry began by ground-driving Snowman, holding the horse on a long rein and walking behind him. But Snowman was used to driving a straight line, so he had no idea how to turn. He wavered like a toddler. Harry persisted, firm but patient. Harry, with the wiry body of a lifelong farmer, knew how to put just the right amount of pressure on the reins. Still, Snowy wove and stumbled. Harry, however, sensed right away that this was a horse who wanted to cooperate, so he continued the way he always persisted with his horses: gently but with confidence.

Once the horse seemed to have gotten the hang of steering, Harry put a saddle on his back, carefully settling it on top of a thick, folded woolen blanket. Calmly, he placed a hand on the horse's shoulder to steady him, then walked a few steps.

Very good! Harry thought as Snowy picked up the pace. To reward the horse, he fished down into a pocket for a stub of carrot. The gray munched on it from the palm of Harry's hand. Harry then reached up and scratched Snowman above his withers, the highest part of his back. The horse arched his neck and curled up his lip, baring his teeth.

"He's laughing," one of the children said. Harry laughed, too. When he scratched the same spot a second time, Snowy laughed again.

The horse was starting to trust him. Harry knew from experience that once horses trusted you, they would soon become your ally.

After the horse seemed to have gotten the hang of steering, Harry put a saddle on his back. The next challenge was to get on top of Snowman. Snowy had pulled a plow but had never been ridden by a human. Most horses' instincts are to throw a rider *off*. That's because in the wild, predators jump onto a horse's back in order to attack them. A horse defends himself by trying to throw the predator off, then using his greatest asset— his speed—to run away. So how was a horse to know that the weight of a person on his back wasn't some kind of predator, like a mountain lion?

Harry knew that even a quiet horse could be unpredictable when mounted. He led Snowman to a mounting block, a large wooden box with steps that helps a rider climb up on a horse. Then, with the grace of a cat, Harry swung up into the saddle. Gently, he landed in the seat, his body tightly coiled. His touch was light; he held himself carefully balanced.

The horse danced a jig, first to one side, then the other. Harry waited, poised. Snowy felt tense underneath him. Uncertain. Clearly, Snowy wasn't used to having anyone atop his back. Harry slowly settled deeper into the saddle. He clucked, using the command that he had taught the horse meant "go forward." One of the gray's ears flicked back, listening.

After a moment's hesitation, Harry felt Snowman's back relax, accepting his presence. He nudged with his heels and the horse started off at a plodding walk. Harry responded with a signal of trust: he let the reins slide out between his fingers. Most riders hold tight reins, to control the horse. Now, if the gelding startled and took off, Harry would have no way to stop him. But Snowman responded to Harry's trust by stretching his neck, and lowering his head.

Harry relaxed into the saddle. He gave Snowman a pat on the shoulder and praised him with a smile. Again, Snowy's well-formed ears flicked back.

This horse—an auction reject who'd been on his way to the slaughterhouse—was looking more promising than Harry had expected. He would make a good pleasure horse for someone—maybe one of the timid riders at the Knox School. Snowman was like an old teddy bear. He was a nice, big horse. As he continued to fatten up, filling out his ribs and bony haunches, his soft, broad back was perfect for a child to climb on. He could easily carry one of the older girls.

Over the next few weeks, Harry rode Snowman in the ring and around the countryside. The horse proved steady and sure-footed. His preferred pace was the walk, and he had to be coaxed even into a dull trot.

Every morning, as soon as Harry came out to the barn,

Snowman blasted out three loud whinnies. Always exactly three. Harry had to chuckle—on this old chicken farm, Snowy had taken on the role of family rooster.

After three weeks, a nice speckled pattern had emerged from the horse's coat. His mane had been detangled and trimmed to a reasonable length. His tail was silky. Harry thought he looked respectable enough to fit in at the stable at the Knox School. As a trial, Harry put one of his own kids up on the horse's back. The gray plodded gently around the ring, while Harry walked alongside.

By the beginning of March, Harry knew the horse was ready to move to the school. He was as nervous as a proud father taking his son to football practice. He wanted Snowman to make a good first impression.

CHAPTER 3

LAND OF CLOVER

ST. JAMES, LONG ISLAND, 1956

Clean, trimmed, and with his mane and tail glossy, Snowman had already come a long way. His wounds had healed, and his coat now glowed.

Harry and Snowy hacked the five miles from the de Leyer farm down to the school, riding at a pleasant pace across open fields. The land around St. James was hilly and wooded. Up near Harry's farm, there were other small farms and modest houses, many of them owned by immigrants. He passed the small businesses in town, like the general store that sold candy and treats. As the trails led closer to the water, the country lanes grew quieter. Seagulls swooped overhead, and the water tower stood out against the blue sky.

Before long, Harry caught sight of the gates that marked the entrance to the Knox School.

Harry led the horse through the arched entrance into the school's grand stable, just inside the front gates. Knox didn't look like your average high school. Its huge brick Georgian house, stables, and grounds resembled a country manor for the wealthy. And in fact, the students who attended the school were just that: wealthy. Here and there, girls in uniforms walked back and forth in twos and threes—lucky students who were being educated in a manner befitting their fortunate backgrounds. Behind the school's tall gates was a place of luck and privilege.

Inside the stable, Harry gave Snowman a pat on the neck and fished in his pocket for a carrot. He could understand how the big horse must feel. Harry remembered how he had felt the first time he set foot on the snazzy grounds of Knox, self-conscious in a necktie and bashful about his broken English.

Harry settled Snowman into one of the empty stalls loaded with fresh straw. The gray-shingled stable was shaped like a horseshoe, overlooking a wide courtyard. It was lined with horse stalls, with double Dutch doors that faced inward onto a covered track. It was quite a contrast to Harry's humble stables at home.

The horse would like this stable at Knox—with its semicircular shape, the animals could see one another, as well as any activity in the courtyard, from any of the stalls. Snowman was a social animal; he liked to be around people and other horses. The girls of the Knox School might be to the manner born, but out at the stable, around the horses, they relaxed and were friendly and happy, like any other kids. Harry thought the old teddy bear would like his new home.

By the time Harry bought Snowman, in 1956, time had erased the exact details of the horse's birthplace and parentage. Snowman brought no backstory except the one inscribed on his body. The cups in his back molars told that he was almost nine years old. The cuts on his knees suggested that he'd once been in some kind of accident. Across his broad chest, the hair was rubbed away—signs of being yoked to a heavy load. The stains, the matted tail, and the unclipped legs and muzzle indicated neglect. The missing shoe and thin frame hinted at an owner who'd refused to pay to maintain an unwanted horse.

But beneath all these physical marks, this horse still carried the story of his bloodlines. The broad chest and strong cannons perhaps originating in the elegant Percherons of France. Even better hidden, in his small, well-set ears and the proud look in his eyes (often described as "the look of eagles"), he carried the mark of a Thoroughbred, and bloodlines that could be traced all the way back through England to the Godolphin Arabian and the desert sands of Morocco.

Most likely, he'd been bred and born down a country lane somewhere, in a big white Amish barn, on the straw-filled bed of a foaling stall.

On horse farms, foals stay with their mothers as sucklings until they are about six months old. At that age, a young foal is weaned. Separated from their broodmares (female horses), weanlings are still small and relatively easy to handle. A weanling learns to be handled by people—first growing accustomed to a person's touch, next to a halter, and eventually to a bridle and bit.

Yearlings are generally put out to pasture to play freely. But when a horse turns two, his training for a life of work begins. Amish handlers first train a horse to voice commands: *ho* for stop, *easy* for slow down, and *break* to change pace.

Once a horse understands commands, he is broken to harness. First to the yoke around the neck. Then to the bridle and reins. And last, to the harness shafts.

Each step takes patience. After that, the training starts. The farmer follows behind the horse, practicing simple walking, stopping, and turning. Eventually, the farmer ties a big rubber tire to the end of a rope and lets the horse get used to pulling it behind him. By the time a horse has reached his third year, he should be trained to work, although he does not reach his full potential until age five.

With good care, a modern pleasure horse can often be ridden well into his twenties, and often lives to thirty or forty years old. But this was not true in the era when horses were used as beasts of burden. The traditional American workhorse's useful life was short. After age ten, its career was finished.

Treated like a servant of humans, and bred for its ability to work hard, the horse used to be considered a "living machine" rather than a being with feelings. In fact, when you think about it, our language is full of examples of thinking of horses as engines; we describe a hard worker as a "workhorse" and a car's engine as having "horsepower." In the early twentieth century, little sentimentality was attached to these creatures. A horse that could no longer work was a horse that could be—and usually was—discarded.

Historically, the United States had long been proud of its equines. Before cars, the horse was an essential part of American workforces. Horses cleared and tilled the land, fought in battles, and pulled heavy loads into cities. Through the late 1800s, the American west not only supplied workhorses for the U.S. Army—it even became the top producer of military horses in the whole world. But the horse remained underappreciated. Often, it was subject to overwork, even abuse.

By the late nineteenth century, the conditions in large cities were considered filthy and dangerous. Progressives wanted to clean up cities by promoting a cleaner and more orderly environment. Horses were at the center of these cleanup projects. The new steam, electric, and internal combustion engines were seen as the wave of the future, while horses were considered dirty and prone to accidents. Their manure was a major contributor to urban filth and a cause of disease.

The original mission of the American Society for the Prevention of Cruelty to Animals (ASPCA), founded in April 1866 by Henry Bergh, was to enforce anti-cruelty regulations for horses. Bergh believed that "mercy to animals meant mercy to all mankind." In nineteenth-century America, horses were the most visible symbol of animal abuse. The ASPCA adopted as its mission the enforcement of anti-cruelty regulations designed to protect urban workhorses, noting, "Among the punishable offenses: overuse of the whip, driving an injured horse, furious driving . . . , knowingly selling a diseased animal, or killing a horse without a license."

Though the role of the workhorse diminished significantly after the dawn of cars, horses performed important tasks well into the twentieth century. In the 1940s, horse-drawn carts were still seen in cities like Baltimore, Pittsburgh, and New York City. There, the clip-clop of hooves on pavement announced the arrival of the junk peddler, the ragman, and the fruit-and-vegetable cart. Throughout cities, the milkman's horse knew the route so well that he would pause at the next stop and wait patiently, unattended, as the milkman ran back and forth across the street to deliver his bottles. It was in these jobs that the horse-driven conveyances lasted the longest.

By the mid-twentieth century, the horse business had

shrunk considerably from its heyday, but its basic setup was still in place. Horses were born and raised on farms or western ranches, auctioned off to dealers who served as middlemen, then sold to individual owners. Noble steed, heroic beast, partner for man—the horse fulfilled all those functions. But the average horse was born and bred to serve humans—harnessed to drag a burden behind him until his useful days were over. In the horse business, the animals had a purpose, and that purpose was to work for human beings. Sentiment, sadly, had no place in the transaction.

Whether Snowman knew it or not, his second chance at life—as the brand-new lesson horse at the Knox School— came about because of one unpredictable chance encounter. For all of the hundreds, thousands, and untold millions of horses who were tossed away like trash as soon as they reached the end of their working lives, here was one who crossed paths with the right man at the right moment.

As with every horse, Snowman's melted-chocolate eyes hid the secret of his thoughts; but right away, when he arrived at the Knox School, he seemed to appreciate his good fortune. From his first day on the job, Snowman carried even the most timid beginner with the gentle care of a four-legged nanny.

In his eight years on earth, Snowman had pulled a plow, suffered neglect, and—almost—been given up for slaughter, then adopted by the de Leyers, nursed back to health, and turned into a riding horse. As he gazed out over the courtyard from his new digs, a roomy box stall in the grand Knox stables, the horse must have been struck by a sense of wonder at his good fortune.

CHAPTER 4

A SCHOOL FOR YOUNG LADIES

THE KNOX SCHOOL, ST. JAMES, LONG ISLAND, 1957

Bonnie Cornelius probably would have died of sheer boredom at the Knox School if it weren't for riding in the afternoon. Everything about Knox felt *heavy*. The paneled front doors opened into a vestibule draped with long, dusty curtains; dark oil paintings stared from the walls, and an ornate chandelier dripped light over the spiral staircase. And between its plush library and its stuffy dining room, the place looked more like a museum or an old mausoleum than a place for teenage girls.

Riding allowed her to escape from life in the big brick dormitory.

The 1950s was a time of drag racing, soda fountains, and poodle skirts, but Knox, an all-girls boarding school, was like an artifact from another era. Knox girls' days were strictly on a schedule: from wake-up, room inspections, and a proper breakfast to dinner, evening study hall, and lights-out. The curriculum was traditional. Music and history, Latin and French. The girls started the school year in summer uniforms, and no matter the weather on the last day of October, they were required to switch to their winter equivalent: navy blue blazers sporting the school's insignia and itchy wool skirts that hung modestly below the knee. They all wore white cotton socks that slouched around their ankles and scuffed lace-up saddle oxfords. Every night, the girls had to change into matching dresses for dinner. Bonnie hated the dinner dresses, instead craving the trousers she could wear astride the Knox School horses.

The dining room was paneled in dark wood, with fireplaces at each end, taller than the girls' heads. Old hunting prints and portraits of people from the past covered the walls. Through the French doors that overlooked the terrace, students could glimpse the beach at Stony Brook Harbor. Meals were plain and hearty. Seated at the head of each table, schoolmistresses carefully scrutinized the use of each knife and fork, as well as the topics chosen for conversation. Every meal, but especially dinner, was a lesson in manners.

Every moment of a Knox schoolgirl's day was considered an opportunity for self-improvement. Little room remained for relaxation or even just plain fun. If a housemother saw a girl sitting with her legs crossed at the knees, she would remind her that Knox girls cross their legs at the ankles. Even off campus, the girls were told, they were ambassadors for the Knox School. Excellent manners were expected.

On the Long Island Rail Road, a Knox girl was easy to spot by her long wool coat and white gloves. While many of the girls hailed from the New York area, others came from out west and even abroad. There were glamorous ranchers' daughters from Texas and Idaho, and rich girls from Puerto Rico and Venezuela. Famous names were not uncommon there.

In the manor house, behavior was a subject of public comment. From wake-up to bedtime, the girls were never far from their housemothers' prying eyes. But cultivating the social graces got very dull. Girls skirted the rules by slinking out to the woods to run around and gossip, or by inviting boys to sneak onto the campus after hours. Students were frequently punished for infractions small and large; the punishments ranged from losing permission to leave the campus to being confined to one's dorm room, allowed out only for classes and meals. All in all, life at Knox was very regimented, extremely proper, and often boring.

Bonnie Cornelius grew up riding horses near her home in Buffalo, where she was a good student at a private school for girls. But her home life, with her father and stepmother, was stressful. When she was a freshman in high school, she discovered boys, and her grades dropped. Her parents weren't thrilled. They decided to send her to Knox, where the adjustment was a shock in many ways. Far from home, she was disappointed to find that the classes were less rigorous than at her old school. At Knox, it was as if manners were prized over intelligence. The living conditions were odd to her as well. Upstairs, the enormous bedrooms of the manor house had been converted into Madeline-style dormitories: five twin beds lined the walls of her shared bedroom, along with five dressers and five desks.

Every girl felt watched. The school's principal was a strict older woman who kept a close eye on the students at all times. The expression on her face always seemed to say, "What have you done wrong now?" The girls had no privacy and little freedom, and the teachers felt free to criticize them about every little thing.

Even weekends were given over to self-improvement. On Sunday nights, for their cultural education, the students had to attend music concerts by string quartets. For these, the hard, straight-backed dining room chairs were arranged in rows. Wearing their dinner dresses and school blazers, the girls were expected to sit up straight, not slump against their chair backs, and, of course, to cross their legs only at the ankles. All while struggling not to allow the music to lull them to sleep.

On weekdays, sports started at two o'clock. The girls raced out of the dorm, then headed up the grassy lane toward the barn or fields. Every girl was required to participate. Besides horseback riding, the girls could choose tennis, field hockey, or basketball. Those in the riding program pulled on their riding garb and hurried up the hill to the stables, looking forward to seeing their favorite teacher, Harry de Leyer, whom they called Mr. D.

As they approached, Harry could hear their laughing and chatting. Rarely was one late. Some were passionate about the sport of horseback riding. Others were beginners who were just giving it a try. The five-day girls, the ones who chose to ride every school day, were the most skilled. The members of the riding club—Wendy Plumb, Bonnie Cornelius, Jackie Bittner, Ann Mead, and Kitsie Chambers—were the most passionately dedicated. These girls would look for *any* excuse to come down to the stables. A few would even show up on weekend afternoons when Harry was feeding, offering to lend a hand. In return, Harry gave them extra opportunities to ride. Up at the barn, the atmosphere was rigorous but fun and can-do. An everyone-pitch-in spirit prevailed.

Horsemanship promoted posture, grace, and confidence

while also providing exercise and fresh air. At an all-girls school, there were opportunities to play other sports but perhaps none that provided the exhilaration, challenge, and freedom of riding. Certainly none that allowed girls to participate in a sport that was fast, dangerous, and thrilling.

Horseback riding was equally popular with boys and men at that time. In fact, girls experienced much more equality with boys in riding than in other sports. Girls wore breeches and boots instead of tunics or dresses, got muddy and dirty, and often took dramatic spills. Sprains, concussions, and broken bones were thought to go with the territory. Horseback riding afforded girls a unique opportunity—it was considered "feminine" and socially graceful, and at the same time, it was exciting and rough-and-tumble.

In Harry de Leyer's stables, the rules were different from those in the rest of the school. The riding program provided a place where girls could escape the scolding and the good manners. Among a faculty of dour, serious women, Mr. D stood out. He was younger, more fun, and almost a big brother–like figure. Harry was not worried about the girls' dress or manners, their deportment or social etiquette. He wanted to make riders out of them.

Bonnie Cornelius was one of Mr. D's best riders—quick to lend a hand around the barn, always one of the first to arrive and one of the last to leave.

In the narrow track that ringed the inside of the circular stable courtyard, Mr. D set up fences for the girls to jump. Some days, he'd keep raising the fences higher and higher. One by one, the girls would peel away, until only the boldest were left. Other days, he'd saddle up and take them galloping out in the fields, looking for natural obstacles—like tree trunks or small streams—to jump. From the school, the group could ride all the way to the beach or into St. James—though the girls got demerits for leaving the school grounds without permission. Harry had noticed that teenagers and horses were the same: you couldn't keep them cooped up for too long.

Riding instructors typically stand in the middle of the ring, calling out instructions to their students from the ground. Mr. D preferred to saddle up and ride alongside them. He'd holler his lessons above the cold wind whistling in from the ocean. In the ring, he raised the jumps higher and shouted, "You got it! You got it!" He saw the shine that came into the girls' eyes when they conquered their fears.

The girls learned manners and deportment, Latin and French, from their mistresses. It was under Mr. D's friendly but exacting eye that they learned courage.

You never knew what life would throw your way. Harry was determined to teach his girls to be brave, to be tough. Out in the field, over the outside course, the girls flew, balanced in their stirrups at a fast gallop, wind whipping into their faces. Harry liked nothing better than leading the girls on a breakneck gallop across woodland and field, riding in a pack, taking fences as they came, adapting seat and balance to uneven terrain. These were the skills he wanted for his girls. He couldn't help but notice how the girls' fancy, rigidly controlled lives made them timid.

Harry's life had taught him that sometimes courage is necessary. Not manners, not breeding and white gloves and nice coats, but the bravery to do what is required of you when the going gets tough.

Harry's own teenage years hadn't exactly been ones of

privilege. But growing up during the war years had taught him something about courage—and endurance. He knew that the hardships he'd faced during the war were nothing compared to the suffering others had endured. It would forever pain him to think about the St. Oedenrode tailor who had once altered school uniforms for young Harry. The Jewish tailor had been forced to wear a yellow star, and had survived the war only by hiding underground in a sealed concrete tank meant to store cow manure for fertilizer. A friend of Harry's had helped blow up a train bridge to impede Nazi movement, and he had paid the ultimate price: transport to a concentration camp, from which he had never returned. Harry's own father had been targeted by the Nazis and had spent the last couple of years of the occupation in hiding, visiting his oldest son only rarely and in the dark of night. Harry had grown up understanding that life was far from easy.

In 1940, when the Nazis invaded Holland, everyone followed the war's progress by listening to the radio. When Rotterdam fell, only seventy miles away, his father came to the school to gather up Harry and his brothers, and took the whole family—his mother and all twelve of his brothers and sisters—to a small two-room cottage out in the country. There, they had huddled together, listening to the radio reports of the Nazis' progress toward St. Oedenrode. Five days later, the family emerged and returned to a town under Nazi control, and a world forever changed.

Quiet but determined, Harry's family fought back in their own way. The German army had commandeered all the valuable food and supplies in the area. They took the best for themselves and rationed out meager supplies to the Dutch people whose homeland they'd just invaded. People had scarcely enough to eat. And what they had was of poor quality. The priest in charge of Harry's school did not have enough food to feed his students and asked Harry's father, a brewer, for grain from his hidden stores. In the dark of night, they sealed wheat and rye into beer barrels and loaded them onto a horse-drawn cart.

Thirteen-year-old Harry was chosen to drive the horse cart the thirty miles back to the school, in the hopes that a young boy on a beer wagon would attract little notice. Harry drove that route at least half a dozen times, holding the reins steady as he approached the armed checkpoints. Surly Nazis stared at him, then let him pass since he was just a skinny kid driving an old wagon through town. Courage and a view of the world seen from atop a horse—the two would forever be linked in Harry's mind.

Now, as a riding instructor, Harry pushed the girls to find and surpass their own limits. One November weekend, he took them to the Junior Olympics, a contest in which teams from all the local riding schools competed. The best horses and best riders were chosen to compete.

Of course, Snowman was not among the selected horses. He was too slow and quiet to be included in the competition, and he did not know how to jump. He stayed behind in the barn, watching curiously as the girls scurried around, preparing the chosen horses, and whickering a soft goodbye as his new stablemates loaded up on the van and headed to the show. At the competition, Bonnie rode Chief Sunset, who was famous for his grumpy temper. In the arena during the warm-up before the competition started, the horse refused a jump, in what's called a "dirty stop": the horse skids to a halt after the rider has already risen in the stirrups and shifted her weight forward. It is very difficult to stay mounted when this happens. This time, Bonnie was thrown. Frustrated with Bonnie for "letting" the horse stop, Harry prepared to get on himself, ready to teach Chief Sunset a lesson.

"We feed these horses," Harry often liked to say. "We groom them, clean their stalls, and tend to them when they are sick. And all we ask of them is to jump. So *make* them jump." Harry took the reins from Bonnie, swung into the saddle, and galloped toward the fence.

Oftentimes, riders are slightly afraid of jumping, and a horse has a fine-tuned sense of his rider's underlying fears. When the rider is afraid, the horse is afraid, too, and will hang back, reluctant on the approach. But when Harry sat astride and confidently approached a fence at a gallop, horses *knew* he meant business. Bonnie watched Harry approach the fence at a good clip; she saw Harry rise up in the stirrups, keeping his legs and heels firmly pressed into the horse's sides, the signal that means *go forward*.

But at the last second, Chief Sunset ducked his head and skidded to a stop. Just as Bonnie had, Harry came unglued, flew out of the saddle, and landed in the dirt. Harry stood up, dusted himself off, and chuckled. Undeterred, he climbed aboard and tried again. This time, prodded by Harry's swift application of the whip before takeoff, the horse jumped the fence. Harry dismounted, handed the reins to Bonnie, and nodded toward the fence—it went without saying that she was going to try again.

Whenever Harry fell, the students gently poked fun at him. But he didn't mind. That was the great thing about Mr. D; he never acted above the girls. Sometimes, Bonnie and the girls would be sore the next morning, but Mr. D had taught them that you always get back in the saddle.

A Spanish proverb says, "It is not enough for a man to know how to ride; he must know how to fall." Harry de Leyer knew how to ride, and he knew how to fall. He taught his girls the same lesson. It was not the trip into the dust that mattered; it was the way the girls got back on and rode again.

Despite the school's stuffy environment, the girls made de Leyer laugh and helped him feel at home. And Snowy had made a good transition to the barn at Knox, charming the girls with his calm, friendly manner. He was popular with the girls, who often stopped by to feed him a carrot or sugar cube, but they never saw him as one of the best horses in the barn. Among the other horses and Thoroughbreds that belonged to these wealthy girls, the big gray gelding certainly stuck out—but Harry admired his ability to seem unbothered by it.

He and Snowy had a lot in common that way.

One day, after a riding excursion at a neighboring estate, Mr. D gave them all a ride back into town in the van. The girls giggled as they climbed into the back and sat down in the straw. The air was warm and heavy with the scent of horses and hay as the beat-up old vehicle rattled along the streets of St. James. They were all going to miss their dinner, so on the way home, Mr. D took the hungry girls out to dinner in a local diner, where they spent the meal excitedly chatting about the day's ride. No dreary housemothers, no lessons in etiquette. Just hamburgers and lively discussion—an opportunity to feel like ordinary teens. In a life filled with string quartets and stiff, white-glove social events, laughter and chatter at a hamburger joint with Mr. D were special treats.

Back at the stables, the girls were bone-weary, but they helped unload the van, put the horses away, and stow all the tack, or riding equipment. At last, their day over, they said good night and trudged back to the manor house to confide their memories in their diaries.

In the morning, the girls would get up and put on their scratchy wool skirts and cotton socks and saddle oxfords. They would sit with ramrod-straight posture in the stuffy rooms of the manor house, where the light leaked in through windows half-covered by heavy damask drapery. They would decline verbs in Latin and submit to the housemistresses' questions and commentary during their meals.

Then, at two o'clock in the afternoon, they would rush up the hill to the barn, and the routine would start again. Up on the backs of horses, the girls would unlock their inner lionesses.

The two-legged teacher would join forces with his four-legged teachers, and have an influence that would last the girls for the rest of their lives.

CHAPTER 5

HOLLANDIA FARMS

ST. JAMES, LONG ISLAND, SPRING 1956

Snowman's winter and spring in the stables at Knox School passed happily. Through lessons and trail rides, the girls quickly grew loyal to the sweet, brown-eyed horse. As the weather warmed, the girls had permission to ride down to the beach after their lessons. To their delight, they discovered that Snowman loved swimming. Many of the horses hesitated at the water's edge or took a few steps in, only to paw and stamp, but Snowman waded past them until the water was chest-deep. Neck stretched forward and nostrils flaring, he'd plunge ahead. In a moment, his hooves took off from the sandy shoals. And just like that, he was waterborne. When the beach was crowded with girls and swimming horses, the sounds of splashing and laughter filled the air.

At the end of May, the school year drew to a close. The dogwoods ringing the fields bloomed flaming pink. In the summer, to save money, the school grounds—including the stables—were shut down. Every summer, when the Knox students left,

Harry would move the school horses back to his own farm on Moriches Road.

This was the time of year when money would get tight in the de Leyer household. If he'd had more space at home, he could have continued with lessons over the summer. But Harry's own tiny property had just a few stalls and a small paddock. Not enough space for a proper riding stable. The Knox stable was three times the size of his.

As the 1956 school year drew to a close, Harry faced a familiar situation: a few of the horses would have to go. This problem was typical of riding academies, camps, and dude ranches all over the country. When the season ended, the extra horses were sold, often going back to the same auctions they had been purchased from.

Sadly, Harry faced the fact that he needed a buyer for one horse. He had a feeling it should be Snowman, the big gray. As kind as he was, he didn't have the skill or flash to carry the girls to their school competitions and shows.

The horse had grown used to his roomy box stall at Knox. Every morning, Snowman would greet Harry with his trademark three loud whinnies, and each time a girl passed his stall, he seemed to give her a playful wink and a nod. Would one of the girls' wealthy families want to buy Snowman?

Deep down, Harry knew the horse just wasn't the kind they went for. The girls preferred the regal Thoroughbreds, like Wayward Wind. Windy had a fine, shiny coat and a silky mane and tail. Her coloring was a deep chestnut, and her white markings—a white blaze down her face, and four white forelegs (known as a horse's *stockings*)—made her stand out. Harry had bought her for very little money and slowly nursed her back to health. Now she was a sweet-natured beauty. The students loved to show her, often bringing home blue ribbons. Riding Windy, a girl really made an impression when she entered the ring.

Snowman was similar in size to Windy, as he stood at 16.1 hands (an equestrian "hand" is four inches, or the width of an average man's hand, and is counted from the ground to the withers, at the top of a horse's back). But his broad chest and heavy-boned legs, all qualities that were bred into workhorses, were not attributes that would appeal to a horse show judge in the way that Windy's sleeker form would.

Nevertheless, Harry kept looking, hopeful to find Snowman a buyer. The horse was reliable and dependable. More than that, he was a gentle four-footed friend. Snowy had the reputation of being the easy horse, the quiet horse, the one you rode if you needed a little help. Even a timid girl could ride this horse without fear. He was the horse you relaxed on after your hard lesson was over, riding bareback down to the beach. The horse you moved past once you got a little better. The horse you were proud not to have to ride anymore, the friendly kid brother who kicked around the stable but got no respect.

Most of the girls were looking for jumpers. Harry had tried trotting Snowman over poles on the ground, but the horse would not pick up his feet. He was clumsy. He just did not have the makings of a jumper. Some horses were born to jump, and others stayed earthbound.

Sure, this horse was a plodder, but Harry still respected his gentle heart.

With no prospect of a buyer for the horse, Harry brought Snowman back to his home stables on Moriches Road. Years ago, his father had taught him a lesson that he'd never forget: that every able-bodied horse on a working farm had to earn his keep. Feeding hay and grain to an animal who had no job and was just growing fat in the barn ... *ach* ... if Harry were that sentimental, he might as well give up now. That was not a way to keep a horse business afloat. And he and the family desperately needed money.

Then, just as Harry was starting to run out of options, a local doctor showed up on Moriches Road, looking for a quiet mount for his twelve-year-old son. The doctor was not a horseman, but he lived on a neighboring farm. He wanted a dependable horse. Nothing flashy. A horse that would be gentle and safe.

Harry smiled and brought the man back to the stable.

I have *just* the right horse, Harry said.

Around back, one of the de Leyer children led Snowman out of the stall, and the horse stood quietly with a rope tossed over his neck, not even clipped into the crossties. The doctor was impressed. This was exactly the kind of calm, friendly horse he was looking for.

After a brief discussion, the two men shook hands. Harry sold Snowman to Dr. Rugen for $160, with just one condition: if the doctor ever wanted to part with the horse, he had to give Harry a chance to buy him back.

The next day, Harry loaded Snowman into the van to take him to his new owner's farm. Snowman's coat shone from grooming and good food. His wounds had healed. The only traces of his past were the places on his shoulders where his coat had been rubbed off by the stress of pulling the plow.

The de Leyer children ran out to say goodbye. They waved as Harry lowered the ramp to the trailer, and the horse clip-clopped up the incline. They knew they would miss Snowman, but their father reassured them that he was going to a good home.

Dr. Rugen's farm was only a few miles away, past farms and potato fields crisscrossed by quiet country lanes. It wasn't long before Harry returned, the trailer now empty.

Harry felt satisfied that he had made a good deal. The horse was in good hands now. The doctor had seemed a sensible man, Harry thought. His pasture was pleasant and grassy.

But still, deep down, it bothered him to let the horse go. Until then, he'd given Snowman a decent home, hay to eat, clean water, good treatment. It was sad to sell a horse who had felt like a member of the family.

Whenever Harry had to find a new home for a horse, he took the task seriously. In fact, it was a task he'd been doing since he was a young man. If he closed his eyes and thought back to his home in Holland, he could still remember the first time he'd done it. When the Germans surrendered the horses they had stolen from Dutch farmers during the war, Harry, a member of a horseback riding club, was assigned the job of examining each horse. No one would ever know exactly what ways the Nazis had used these horses to carry out their atrocities. When the horses came back to St. Oedenrode, in many ways they resembled the Dutch people: once healthy and shiny, now gaunt, with new scars on their bodies and a wilder look in their eyes. But like the people, they had survived.

With his father and brother, Harry had examined each of these horses, picked up their feet, looked over their legs, checked their eyes and wind, their tails and backs. Every once in a while, they recognized a horse—one with distinctive markings—and could return it to the original owner. But most of them came without pedigrees and would be going to new homes. Young Harry felt the weight of each decision. For each horse, he chose a new owner. For each farmer, that horse might make the difference between success and failure, between helping the farm flourish, or losing it.

Harry would never know exactly where Snowman came from, but he knew how it felt to be displaced, neglected, and undervalued—and yet to *still* face the future with ears pricked forward.

Yes, a farm nearby and a boy looking for a quiet mount. The doctor's friendly home was a perfect new space for Snowman.

Still, on the evening of the gentle horse's departure, sadness hung in the air as Harry did his rounds and checked the other horses. Thinking of Snowy, it was hard for Harry not to feel a lonely pit settle deep in his stomach. He thought of his mother and father and all his brothers and sisters left behind in Holland; he thought of his brown mare Petra, who had made him proud in jumping competitions; and for a moment, he leaned on his pitchfork and looked out across the darkening horizon. The evening was quiet, with nothing but the sound of faraway birdsong and chirping crickets in the air.

But soon he straightened up and set himself back to work. Here he was, on his own little patch of ground, his own Hollandia Farms, taking care of his wife and family. Harry so missed the gray's three friendly whinnies trumpeting from the barn like an equine cuckoo clock. Still, he brushed aside the hollow feeling inside. He knew that if he was going to make a go of it in the horse business, he couldn't get himself attached to every old plow plug that came through the barn.

CHAPTER 6

HOW TO MAKE A LIVING AT HORSES

HIGH POINT, NORTH CAROLINA, 1951

Harry was twenty-two years old when he and his wife, Johanna, rode the Dutch flagship *Volendam* into the port of Hoboken, New Jersey. The year was August 1950. They were part of a wave of about two million new postwar immigrants who landed in the United States from Europe at that time.

The early 1950s was a time of brash new developments that would forever change the face of the country. There was the advent of television, the first credit card was introduced, and the company Xerox manufactured the first copy machine. A gallon of gasoline cost eighteen cents. Change was happening all over the country—and the world.

It was also a fearful time. The Korean War had started. Cold War tensions were rising. Technological changes were arriving at a breathtaking pace. But like generations of immigrants before them, Harry and Johanna were undeterred by the uncertainties of the future. They knew hardship firsthand, and they arrived with the intention of building a good life for themselves in this new land.

The ship's six-day journey across the ocean had been rough and choppy. Harry spent most of it curled up seasick below-decks until they reached Hoboken, just across the Hudson River from New York City. As the young newlyweds stepped off the boat, it was hard *not* to be overwhelmed by all the unfamiliar sights and sounds. Before arriving in Hoboken, Harry and Johanna had passed through Ellis Island, where immigration inspectors had cleared their papers and performed a brief medical exam. At the loud, clanging port in Hoboken, the customs inspectors cracked the lid of the small wooden crate that held all of the young couple's belongings. They did not have much. Harry's worn leather saddle and his tall riding boots took up much of the space. Harry and Johanna stepped into their new homeland without a backward glance.

When the young couple arrived in America, they had only $160 between them. Their clothes were plain, they spoke little English, and they carried little with them, but they had a bright look in their eyes. A look that was fixed on the future. They boarded the train going south, headed toward a new life that they were determined to embrace.

Before the war, it would have been unthinkable that Harry, the oldest son of a prosperous brewer, would someday be standing with his wife on the dock in Hoboken, New Jersey, with little more than his hopes and dreams and one small wooden crate. But for the war, Harry's future would have been assured. Growing up, he'd believed that he would lead a life much like his father's. While he wasn't interested in the brewery business his dad ran, he loved the farm they lived on. As the oldest son, it had always been assumed he would take it over.

The war had changed all that. The farms needed to be rebuilt, and the economy was sagging. In his boyhood, Harry had worked harder than anyone to help his father keep the farm running. The farm and the brewery went hand in hand: the crops fed the animals and provided the hops for the beer. The one couldn't survive without the other. But after the war, without horses to work the land, the fields had lain fallow. The whole farm had fallen into disarray.

Then, a year or two after the war ended, just when things were starting to look a little better, a tornado swept through town, knocking over trees and littering the fields with fallen branches and debris. The next morning, Harry, then eighteen, and his younger brother Jan, thirteen, headed out to clean up their land. Harry took two horses over to a field that needed plowing. Jan took a third horse in the other direction. A short while later, Harry looked up, confused to see Jan's horse galloping toward him unhitched. His brother was nowhere in sight.

Harry left his horses and ran to the next field. When he reached the clearing, he gasped.

There, unconscious, lay Jan. A tree branch had downed an electric wire, and a powerful electric shock had jolted him.

Harry sprinted back to the farmhouse, shouting as he ran. The family poured outside to come to their aid.

Pale and silent, Jan lay in a coma for days. Each day the village doctor came over to check on him. Jan said little, and often just shook his head.

The family watched tensely over the handsome young boy,

hoping for some sign that he would take a turn for the better. They prayed and lit candles, watched and waited. After a few days, Jan opened his eyes and began to speak. It was a slow process, but he would eventually get better, making almost a full recovery. Jan had always been a clever boy. After the accident, he struggled in school. He was still good with the farmwork and the animals, but he was no longer able to learn the way he had.

It had always been expected, by the entire family, that Harry, as the eldest son, would take over the farm. But Jan, like Harry, had always been interested in farming. Harry, who still had so many opportunities ahead of him, could see that Jan was going to need it more than he did.

It was then that Harry's mind started to wander to faraway shores. Harry had always felt attached to his homeland, but he also couldn't help remembering the American paratroopers he had met during the war. Those paratroopers were cocksure and courageous. The young Dutch boys had flocked around the Americans, eager to help them fight the Nazis any way they could.

Now the only soldiers left in St. Oedenrode were dead ones. The field where Harry used to practice his horseback riding had been turned into a graveyard.

Harry would not mind moving far away, to a place where the American soldiers hailed from. Lucky for him, the family of a soldier who'd been in Holland agreed to sponsor him to come to America.

There was only one thing left to do. Back then, Harry had already been sweet on Johanna for years. Her brothers rode with Harry in the 4-H riding club. Johanna was a brown-haired beauty who loved the same things that Harry did—animals, and especially horses. Johanna's sister had already immigrated to America, and when Harry talked about going there, Johanna's eyes shone. She, too, could imagine the fields that stretched out as far as the horizon.

Now, after the long train ride from Hoboken to the southern states of America, the couple was freshly landed on a farm in North Carolina. In spite of the heat and humidity—which was stronger than he had ever known—and in spite of the hard hours of work between sunrise and sunset, Harry and Johanna attacked their new life with the vigor particular to those who have known hardship.

Harry did not mind field work. He'd been doing it all his life. But he missed taking care of animals. Most of all, he missed the horses. He would never forget the flying sensation of jumping, back in Holland, in a huge arena festooned with bunting and bursting with the sounds of a brass band. Those cherished memories helped him get through his long days. As always, Harry wiped his sweaty brow and got on with his work.

In the afternoons, Harry often walked a quarter mile down the road to help out at his neighbor's dairy farm. Calvin Ross ran a small ice business and a farm. He had a gas-powered engine to blow the hay up into the silos, but he used a horse-drawn wagon to pull the corn in from the fields. Harry offered to drive the wagon. He breathed a sigh of relief being back around the animals. The dairy farm, with its predictable rhythms, reminded him of life back home.

At Cal's farm, horses still did much of the work. These were workhorses, though. Not riding horses. Still, Harry couldn't resist saddling one up. Experimenting with all three horses, and building makeshift fences from old posts and rails, Harry found that one of them could even jump a bit. He called the mare Petra, after the beloved horse he had left behind in Holland.

People around town scratched their heads at the sight of Harry and Petra out in the fields. Late in the steamy summer afternoons, North Carolinians liked to relax in the shade with something cold to drink. They couldn't help but stare at Harry as he passed them by, dirty and sunburned from being outside all day, riding in the field on that clunky old plow horse. Still, if a person who knew horses happened by, it was clear from the way the young man sat in the saddle, from the ease in his back, and the light hands on the reins, that he knew how to ride.

Circling around, galloping, and jumping, for a few minutes Harry could forget everything and recapture that feeling of flying. The language he spoke to the horses was mostly silent, but sometimes he muttered a few words in Dutch.

Soon enough, he heard a piece of news that made him smile: a local horse show was coming up. The entry fee was three dollars; it bought a rider the chance to vie for a ten-dollar prize. For Harry and Johanna, three dollars was a lot of money. But riding mattered to Harry, deep down in his bones. He worked so hard all the time, they reasoned, that it couldn't hurt for him to ride in the show. The old plow horse didn't stand a chance, but Harry groomed her as though she were a top Thoroughbred.

Back home in Holland, the very same horses who pulled the plows and carriages were saddled up and ridden to horse shows on the weekends. This seemed normal to Harry. So he dug out his riding breeches and jacket from his suitcase, and Johanna carefully mended and ironed them. He blacked his tall boots and slicked down his hair. With his plow horse Petra in tow, Harry was ready to go.

*   *   *

There are no photographs to record the moment when Harry de Leyer arrived at his first horse show on American soil, in North Carolina. He was riding an old workhorse, and his clothing was correct but simple. But he had taught the horse well, and Harry brought home the blue ribbon and the ten-dollar prize in the open jumper class. Johanna, standing at the railing, was mostly excited about the money, which would help pay for much-needed baby things. They were expecting their first child.

But someone else stood near the railing that day. A savvy Irishman named Mickey Walsh. With his broad smile, white linen jacket, and bow tie, Mickey was a recognizable figure. Irish through and through, the fifty-year-old had wavy gray hair set off by bright blue eyes. Now at the very top of his game, Mickey had recently founded the Stoneybrook Steeplechase in Southern Pines, North Carolina, a horse-centered community not far from the farm where Harry and Johanna worked.

Mickey Walsh had come up the hard way. Born into a family that had been in the horse business for generations, Mickey left home as a young man to seek his fortune in the United States. But he arrived in New York at a time when prejudice against Irishmen abounded. Signs declaring NO IRISH NEED APPLY were emblazoned on shop windows throughout the city. Mickey finally found a job leading out horses in Central Park. He worked his way up, and became a horse boy for some of the grand estates on Long Island, New York.

Mickey Walsh soon became one of the most competitive jumper riders in the country, winning every major championship for a series of rich owners. That day in North Carolina, Harry's grace in the saddle was immediately apparent to an old salt like Mickey. Maybe it takes a rider to know a rider, because Mickey—unfazed by Harry's plow horse mount and provincial Dutch riding habit—recognized him in an instant for what he was: a man with a gift.

After Harry had secured his blue-ribbon rosette and the prize money, the Irishman approached. Harry's understanding of English was still a bit rough, but he recognized the Irish brogue.

"What do you do, young man?" Mickey asked.

"I'm a farmer," Harry replied.

"You're no farmer. You are a horseman. You should be working in horses."

Harry's heart beat a little faster. He could not imagine anything better. Perhaps there were opportunities here, in a land that seemed full of hope and promise. A place not scarred by the war.

Ah, to be working around horses . . .

But he was a family man now; his wife was going to have a baby. Horses were for fun. The work on the farm was where his livelihood lay.

The Irishman looked at him with bright eyes and an open smile.

Harry tried to form the word *no*. But it just wouldn't come to him. He sat astride that old workhorse, holding Mickey Walsh's gaze. For a moment, just one moment, Harry de Leyer allowed himself to imagine a better life. The life he really wanted.

"I don't know if I'm good enough . . . ," Harry said.

"Oh, you're good enough," Mickey said. "I can tell you want

to win more than most people, and believe me, son, that's all it takes."

Riding back to Cal's farm at the end of the day, Harry felt tired but satisfied. He had ten dollars in his pocket, and the words of the older man lodged somewhere deep in his heart.

Harry turned over the words in his mind as he lay down to sleep that night. He couldn't imagine wanting anything more than he wanted to ride.

But he and Johanna were all too aware that their crops on the farm weren't looking good. The summer season had been hot and dry. They needed rain, and a lot of it soon. No rain meant no crops. And no crops meant they'd be out of money.

Johanna was now seven months pregnant. Their start-up capital, the $160 they'd brought from Holland, had been almost exhausted. Meanwhile, the long, hot summer dragged into a dusty, dry fall. Each day, they squinted at the sky, looking for rain that didn't come.

The glossy rows of their farm crops started to shrivel and yellow.

Eventually, Harry and Johanna had to face the truth. The crops were worthless that year. All of their hard work had come to nothing. It was time for them to look for work elsewhere. Harry needed a salary, however small. Anything to keep them afloat.

With all of the changes going on in the American farm economy, it was not a propitious time to be an immigrant trying to make a living in farming. In prewar Holland, the farm and brewery had supported their entire family—but as Harry had quickly learned, the gulf between working as a hired hand and owning your own land was vast. All over the country, droves of young people were leaving the land behind for higher education or factory work. Farms that had been in families for generations were sold off.

Harry and Johanna didn't know what their next move should be, and now they had another mouth to feed. Harry roamed the streets, looking for work. When he'd stepped aboard the ship bound for America, it had never occurred to Harry that he would *not* be a farmer. He'd spent his entire life working the land. But times were changing.

However, Mickey Walsh had kept the young man in mind. Mickey had promised to keep his eye out for work for Harry. So far, there'd been nothing. And just when things were looking bleakest, a call came through. Mickey had recommended Harry for a position across state lines, in a Pennsylvania riding stable. A job in horses. Once again, Johanna and Harry packed up their suitcases and moved on.

CHAPTER 7

THE STABLE BOY

BAKERSTOWN, PENNSYLVANIA, 1951

Soon enough, Harry and Johanna found themselves at the Stirrup Hill Horse Farm, in Bakerstown, Pennsylvania. From morning to night, Harry was working with horses. A jack-of-all-trades at the stable, he did anything and everything: cleaning stalls, feeding the horses, helping the riders who came for trail rides and lessons. He groomed horses to get them ready to ride, and afterward, he cooled them down and led them back to their stables.

He and Johanna had a place to live on the grounds of the stables—just a small apartment. Finally, Harry had a regular paycheck: $35 a week. Even in the early 1950s, though, when the average American salary was about $3,500 dollars a year, Harry's wages were next to nothing. Especially for a growing family. The lean war years had taught Johanna to scrimp and save. She was determined to stretch each dollar as far as she could. Johanna clipped coupons from the newspaper, mended clothes and darned socks, and never let a penny go unaccounted for.

As hard as he worked, Harry still felt that his life was one of ease. Especially compared to the hardships of the war years—the things that he had endured, and the even harder things that he had seen others endure. To be paid to ride horses seemed like incredibly good fortune. Harry worked from the crack of dawn, when he got up to muck the stalls, till after sunset, when he came in, bone-weary and smelling of hay and saddle soap. Despite the work and the meager pay, he had the feeling that, at last, he was doing what he was meant to.

Harry's boss was happy with him; he was good at his job, a hard worker, and serious. Harry kept the stalls clean and banked up with fresh straw, and he groomed all the horses, keeping their manes tidy and their coats buffed to a gloss. Harry even got to ride some of them. His boss had noticed that he had a gift. Harry could calm the nervous horses, handling even the most difficult ones without a problem.

Huge animals with lightning-fast reflexes, horses are built to move quickly. A startled horse will lash out with his hooves and attempt to bolt. Since horses outweigh humans by a power of ten, humans have had to come up with clever ways to calm and control them.

Harry's methods of calming horses were gentler than most. First, he'd stand in front of a horse with his lead rope slack. Most people lack the courage to stand directly in the path of a frightened horse, but Harry had a knack for it. Then he'd look the beast straight in the eye and calmly hold up one hand. His movements seemed to speak to the skittish animals. In response, the horse would usually snort and snuffle. Then it would drop its head and reach its nose forward toward Harry's outstretched palm.

From then on, the horses trusted that Harry—with his patient manner—would do right by them.

Harry did a good job. But Johanna was worried. Thirty-five dollars a week was hardly enough to put food on the table, even with her thrifty ways. Their baby, Joseph, was one by now, and a second baby was on the way. Another ten dollars a week would make a world of difference to the young family.

Harry and Johanna talked it over. He should ask his boss for a raise, they decided. And so, the next day, hat in hand, Harry approached his boss.

"I've been here for a year," he said. "I've worked hard, and I think you like what I do."

Harry's boss had nodded in agreement. The young man *was* a hard worker and one hundred percent reliable. And he was a family man, not off carousing like many of the young stable boys.

"I need a raise," Harry said. "Just ten dollars per week."

The boss didn't even pause long enough to give the impression that he was thinking it over. He said no. Firmly.

"But—"

Harry did not get a chance to finish his sentence. His boss held up his hand. "There are a million more guys like you out there—guys who want to spend their days fooling around on a horse. Not my problem you've got mouths to feed. . . . I can find somebody who will be happy to work for sixty dollars a month."

Harry sighed, heading back to his and Johanna's small apartment. He was disappointed. Still, this past year working with horses had convinced him that he *could* make a living at it.

So Harry called Mickey again and asked him for advice.

By now, Mickey was living the high life, but he had not

forgotten the people who had given him an early break when he was just a horse boy in Central Park.

"I think I've got something for you," Mickey said. "Big farm in Virginia—the wife's Dutch. . . . The man is older and he likes to ride out early in the mornings. A daredevil. She worries he'll get hurt. She wants someone to ride with him."

Virginia. Harry had heard that Virginia was horse country in the United States of America. So he and Johanna loaded up their station wagon. With Joseph tucked into the back seat, they headed off to their new home, a place called Homewood Farms.

Nothing could have prepared Harry and Johanna for the beauty of the grand Homewood Farms estate. The countryside around the city of Amherst, in Virginia's renowned Shenandoah Valley, was storybook beautiful: huge rolling farms and long, tree-lined lanes, with peacocks strutting across the grounds. Set on hundreds of manicured acres, Homewood Farms was a showplace. Rough log smokehouses produced Virginia hams every year, cured and smoked to perfection. Acres of crops yielded fresh produce. In the dairy farm, Jersey cows produced rich milk and butter.

And at the private racetrack at the adjacent Oak Park Farms, the farm's owner—Mr. David Hugh Dillard—ran his Thoroughbreds. Mr. Dillard strutted across his huge plot of land like one of his peacocks—proud and showy. He was proud of his farm, his horses. He even had his own racetrack. Now he wanted to start training some of the horses in the glamorous sport of show jumping.

That was where Harry came in. Harry had initially been hired to accompany Mr. Dillard on his morning rides. But right away, Mr. Dillard put the young man to work doing more. He suggested that Harry might be able to start up a horse business, buying and selling horses. He'd even lend Harry the money to do it.

So soon enough, Harry started buying a few horses. Students from the local high school showed up for riding lessons. Everyone at Homewood liked Harry. The horses whinnied when they saw Harry coming, and the boys and girls followed him like a litter of puppies.

Johanna loved her new home, and she loved Mrs. Dillard, too—the kindly wife of her husband's boss was of Dutch heritage and always showed them the utmost respect. Johanna and Harry's second child, Harriet, was born shortly after they arrived there. Then, like clockwork, a year later, another blond-haired boy, Marty.

Mr. Dillard paid Harry a fair wage, and let him earn additional money from teaching and buying and selling a few horses of his own. Harry's horses were starting to win ribbons at local shows. Life was pleasant; it seemed like a place to settle in and call home.

For Harry, however, it was not enough. As much as he enjoyed living at Homewood, he wanted a home of his *own*. He wanted horses of his own, too.

In St. Oedenrode, back in Holland, the farm and the brewery had belonged to the family. Working for Mr. Dillard, no matter how pleasant, felt like relying on the good graces of others. Harry dreamed of starting a business that was his alone. A proper riding establishment where he could train horses and teach people to ride. But he didn't have the money to do it.

Harry wanted to be his own boss. Working for Mr. Dillard

had given him a taste of the life he wanted, one where he ran his own business and called all the shots. He could not spend his life catering to the whims of rich people.

A short while later, a new proposition came Harry's way: The Knox School for Girls in Long Island, New York, was looking for a new riding teacher. Would Harry be interested?

Now Johanna had three small children to tuck into the back seat, Joseph, Harriet, and Marty; another house to dismantle; and another new life to start from scratch. And who knew what they would find there—up in New York, where neither of them had ever been?

But it looked like a good opportunity, so once more the de Leyers packed up their belongings and moved toward the future.

That was how, six years after his arrival in America, Harry found himself with his own business in St. James, his own horses, and his own tiny piece of land. There were times when he had to make hard choices—which horses to keep and which ones to sell. Selling Snowman had been one of the most difficult decisions, but he could live with it because it was his own choice.

CHAPTER 8

WHERE THE HEART IS

ST. JAMES, LONG ISLAND, MAY 1956

Up before dawn, Harry drank scalding black coffee. Then he slipped into his wooden shoes and headed outside. A few pink streaks lightened the sky.

As the horses heard Harry's heavy shoes clump down the lane, they started to whinny and stamp. Harry still half expected to hear Snowy's familiar nicker among the chorus. But Snowman's stall stood empty. The entire barn seemed empty without him. *Ach*, Harry had a sentimental streak. He struggled when it came to selling his beloved horses. He always missed them when they were gone.

Sure enough, the remaining horses in Harry's stables were restless. They stamped and rustled inside their stalls, weaving back and forth as Harry walked down the barn aisle, tossing flakes of hay and pouring oats into rubber buckets. Slants of early-morning light poured through the barn windows, lighting up the dust motes that hung in the air.

Harry went down the line, calling each horse by its nickname.

An air of calm settled over the barn. German shepherds trotted at his heels as he worked. A few stable cats strutted in the aisle or licked their paws. Harry was the only two-legged critter in the barn, but he looked as much at home there as any of the others.

He loved his quiet early mornings, before the family was up. It was a good time to think. This morning, he was thinking about the big hole Snowman had left in the stable. To Harry, it almost felt like losing a member of the family. But then he chuckled to himself—Johanna was expecting again. That helped him keep things in perspective. Selling Snowman had been sad, but at least it had put a few dollars in his pocket.

And money was what Harry needed.

His mind kept wandering back to the ten dollars he'd won in North Carolina. What if he could make money competing? After all, some of the biggest horse shows in the country were nearby in Long Island. They were mostly filled with Thoroughbred horses. Those creatures were natural athletes whose fine breeding showed in their every move.

With the right horse, why shouldn't Harry compete in these shows, too? He was willing to put in the time to train a beginner. A horse with potential. But even an untrained Thoroughbred could cost thousands. It was hard enough to earn his living by teaching riding at the school; training a champion jumper all by himself—it just didn't seem possible.

Harry had an old photo album with pictures of himself parading through Amsterdam aboard Petra carrying his equestrian club's flag. In those days, he seemed a good bet to make the Dutch Olympic team. But nowadays that album was kept high up on a shelf and rarely looked at. That world was long gone. Now, Harry needed to look toward the future.

As he forked fresh straw into the wheelbarrow and pushed it down the barn aisle, he knew that the desire to ride in shows was still there, a slow-burning ambition that never left him. Harry planned to keep his eye out for the right horse. One that needed some training, but had raw skill. A diamond in the rough.

By the time the round of barn chores was finished, Harry took a last look around, satisfied. Everything was in order, and all was quiet except for the sounds of horses chewing their morning feed. The sun was rising, and Harry heard the kitchen door bang: the children were up. Quiet time was over. Now on to the rest of his day. From the look of the sky, it would be fine weather for riding.

After a few days, Harry wasn't thinking about the big gray gelding quite so much. But one afternoon, he got a call from Snowman's new owner—who was *not* happy. Dr. Rugen complained that the horse had escaped his pasture and trampled his neighbor's fields. Was Harry *sure* the horse wasn't a runaway? Harry reassured the man. Horses are not prone to jumping out of their pastures. Usually, if they're given enough food and water, they're inclined to stay put. Was it possible that the doctor had forgotten to double-latch the gate? A clever horse can nuzzle open a gate if the latch isn't closed tight.

Certainly not, was the doctor's indignant answer. Of course he had latched the gate. The horse had *jumped* out of the pasture.

Harry repeated his advice to make sure to keep the gate

firmly latched shut. He hung up with a chuckle, expecting he would not hear from the owner again.

For those who don't know equines well, it is always a surprise that horses are normally content to stay inside paddocks constructed of post-and-rail fences. It's surprising because those same horses, when entered in jumping competitions, will willingly leap these same fences with a rider aboard. Unlike, for example, deer—which must be restrained by fences fourteen feet high—horses will happily stay inside pastures fenced at three and a half or four feet.

Horses are born with the ability to jump. Jumping helps them get over small obstacles when they are galloping across open terrain. But horse jumping as a sport developed relatively recently. It grew from the European tradition of hunting on horseback. In eighteenth-century France, riders would follow hounds on stag hunts across miles of countryside. Sometimes the riders would have to jump over obstacles along the way: ditches, banks, low stone walls, and small creeks. Eventually, people realized that the thrilling sight of a horse leaping a fence could attract spectators. Soon enough, artificial "fences" were constructed inside the confines of riding arenas. To this day, the obstacles in horse shows are named after natural obstacles found in the fields (like *brush*, *chicken coop*, *ditch*, and *water jump*).

Horses are large creatures—they can weigh over one thousand pounds each! They do not often jump fences on their own. When galloping across a pasture, they may leap playfully over a small ditch or log. But usually they'll stop at a fence. One of the most remarkable things about horses is their willingness to jump for a rider they trust. Though jumping is a natural ability, there is little evidence in nature that a horse will *choose* to leap over things on its own.

That was why Harry assumed that the doctor, an inexperienced horseman, had either forgotten to lock the gate or had a broken section of fence. The idea of an old plow horse taking it in his mind to jump out of the pasture was unheard of! And sure enough, Harry didn't hear back from Snowman's new owner.

For the next few days, that is. One morning when Harry went out to feed, he noticed something unusual out of the corner of his eye. It was a horse, standing loose in the barnyard. A big gray glowing in the dawn light. The horse lifted his head and nickered three times.

Harry peered at the creature before him. Could it really be Snowy?

"What are you doing here, you bandit?" Harry asked, bewildered. He reached out his hand and the gelding took a few steps toward him, stretching his neck to nuzzle Harry's bare palm. His warm breath tickled. Harry would swear he had a pleased-as-punch look on his face.

The sun was just coming up, and the grass fields sparkled with silver dew. As Harry scratched his horse's favorite spot near the withers, he looked thoughtfully out across the fields. His eyes ran along the rows of fences around the stables. They provided no clues as to how the horse had gotten here. Not one was out of place. The gate was firmly latched. Dr. Rugen's property was several miles down the road.

There was no way Snowman could have made it all this way

on his own. Unless . . . Snowman *had* always had an intelligent look in his eyes, ever since that first day at the auction. Harry realized he might have underestimated the gelding. Then again, it still seemed impossible that the sweet, clumsy horse would have made it all this way alone.

Harry shook his head in disbelief as he went to call Dr. Rugen. "I've got your horse," Harry said. "You must have a fence down somewhere. I'll keep him safe until you get here."

"I checked the pasture fence myself yesterday," Dr. Rugen said. "But I'll have another look and be over to fetch him."

The next morning, Harry was thinking about Snowman's great escape as he headed out to the barn. In the stable court-yard, it was still dark. No sign of a loose horse. Looked like the doctor had figured out how to keep the gate latched, Harry figured. He was a little surprised to feel a slight sinking feeling. In a way, he'd hoped Snowman would be back.

A second later, the big horse came into view. He was munching hay, and raised his head at the sight of Harry.

"You . . . again . . . ?"

Snowman looked pleased with himself. It was a drizzly morning, and he had mud on his legs. His forelock swept across his forehead at a rakish angle. His eyes were bright and his ears pricked forward at the sight of Harry. With his broad chest and arched neck's crest, he almost didn't look like a plow horse. As he moved toward Harry, he whinnied a soft greeting.

"Well, we do like having you here, but you can't stay," Harry said, approaching Snowman. He took the horse's head in his arm and stroked the soft part of his muzzle. Snowman made no move to run away. He was as quiet as ever, even standing there loose, not bothering the other horses in the stalls or trying to get into mischief. When Harry walked, Snowman followed him like a puppy, nudging his pocket for a carrot as he walked.

Nothing in the horse's temperament had made Harry think he'd try to run away. After all, Snowman had never tried to stray from the de Leyer barn. But one dissatisfied customer could spread a lot of bad news about a horseman's business. The doctor, though a kind man, was getting crankier. And no wonder. Harry had advertised Snowman as quiet and an easy keeper. Not a runaway jumper.

There had to be a way to make this work. Harry offered to check out the doctor's pasture to see what the problem was.

Rugen's place was typical of small farms in the area. Flat fields that used to grow potatoes. Brown timber fences. Nothing seemed amiss. A nuzzle-proof snap held the gate closed.

Still, Harry walked around the entire fence line, testing each section to see if it would budge. Nothing did.

"You sold me a jumper," the doctor said.

Harry tried to repress a smile, but it was difficult.

The doctor wanted to know what was so funny.

"If I'd have known the horse could jump, I would have charged you more for him," Harry answered.

The doctor did not look amused.

"Consider him a bargain," Harry said, smiling again. It was true that the situation was a *little* funny. Here was a horse that couldn't even jump over a pole lying on the ground—and now he had gone and jumped whole fences back to Harry's stables.

Harry studied the big pasture. It was divided into two parts: one large, one small.

"Can you keep him confined to the smaller pasture at night?"

The doctor nodded, and asked why.

"Well, let's just say he *is* jumping—and I don't see any other way he'd get out. He wouldn't be able to get a running start from in there. Not much more than a couple of strides. That'd make it a much harder jump, and very few horses would do that."

The doctor agreed to give it a try.

Harry sure wouldn't mind finding a horse that could clear four feet with only a couple of strides to get a running start. If he had a horse like that, he'd be schooling him for the Sands Point Horse Show in September.

Harry liked being in charge of his own business, but that meant his budget was only big enough to buy broken-down ex–plow horses, not trophy challengers. And ex–plow horses did not normally jump four-foot fences. Certainly not without a running start.

Harry was puzzled, but he was sure they could get Snowman to stay put now. Harry gave the troublemaker a scratch on the neck before he left.

"Now, stay here, you old bandit," he said. "You're making a lot of trouble."

Harry knew what it felt like to kick around without a real place to call your own. It was hard not to have a soft spot for a horse who wanted to come home that badly. Harry was pretty sure that horses were a whole lot smarter than people gave them credit for.

The next morning, sure enough, Snowman was back at Harry's. And a couple of days later, he turned up again. The doctor *swore* he had kept the horse confined to the small pasture, that no fences were down, that the gate had been double-latched each night. He was reaching the end of his patience. The last thing Harry wanted to do was alienate his neighbors.

Yet again, a few mornings later, Snowman was back. The big gray horse was standing in the middle of the stable courtyard.

First, Harry just stared. Then he started to laugh.

Snowman's head was high. When he saw Harry laughing, he shook his head, rattling the snap on his lead rope. There was no mistaking the pride in the horse's eyes.

Standing in the barnyard, Harry unclipped the tattered lead rope and led Snowman back to a stall. There was more to horses than buying and selling and making money. There is one thing no horseman can ever put a price on, and that is heart.

CHAPTER 9

THE HORSE CAN JUMP

ST. JAMES, LONG ISLAND, 1956

Harry's kids celebrated their favorite's return, playing with him and clambering up on his back to ride. Snowy was always gentle around children, taking care where to put his giant hooves, nuzzling their hands, standing patiently while being groomed. Harry chuckled as Marty hugged Snowy's big leg.

Harry himself had started sitting on horseback when he was two. By the time he was eight, he could keep up with the older riders, jumping high obstacles. Harry remembered the times when everyone else had gone home, when the sky was darkening behind the church in St. Oedenrode, and he remained, bone-sore in the saddle. Harry was working on one move—a flying lead change or a tight turn. He was always trying to improve. Harry knew he could read a horse with just the touch of his fingers and the feel under his seat bones. He knew it absolutely.

Harry wanted his children to grow up just as he had, living and breathing horses. With Snowman, since the doctor had sold him back, his kids were learning to do just that.

Snowman was a perfect children's horse. Still, Harry could not forget the sight of the horse standing in front of him. There were half a dozen five-foot paddock fences between home and the doctor's farm.

Maybe this seemingly unassuming horse was trying to tell him something.

Between riding with the Knox girls and running his own small stable, Harry de Leyer spent so much time on horseback during his first year on Long Island that he often felt the rhythm of a trot even when he was off a horse. He rode so much that he estimated distances not in feet or yards but in horse strides, intuitively knowing how many it would take to reach a far-off pasture fence.

At night, he lay in bed thinking about horses. Harry wanted all his horses to be happy and comfortable. He had always believed you should treat a horse the way you would want to be treated. Simple enough. That rule, learned from his father, had served him well.

To Harry, every new horse that came into the barn was a puzzle to be solved. Snowman was an especially tricky riddle. If the horse could jump big sturdy paddock fences, why had he not shown any particular skill with a rider on his back?

Harry tried to think like a horse. Like other mammals, horses have five senses. Their acute vision, keen sense of smell and hearing, and exquisite sensitivity to touch are all designed to protect them from predators. Since Harry liked to treat horses the way he himself wanted to be treated, he wondered why he should tug on the horse's mouth all the time, like some riders. Harry reasoned that if he had a bit in his *own* mouth, he'd want its use to be as gentle as possible.

A rider must give a horse reason to trust him or her. Horses can "read" subtle changes, such as a slight movement of a rider's lower legs, a tightening of the reins, or an almost imperceptible shift in balance. And a horse and rider who are working well together will communicate in a fine-tuned nonverbal language— a sort of equestrian Braille. Messages are telegraphed from rider to horse in a way that, at its highest level, is almost invisible to a spectator.

All horses have some ability to jump, but most horses are not born to be jumpers. Three physical qualities factor into a horse's ability to clear high obstacles: speed, spring, and balance. Speed and spring are inborn. Balance, on the other hand, must be taught.

Harry knew Snowman had spring. The horse had demonstrated that already by leaping paddock fences with next to no running start. But the power needed to pull a plow was *nothing* like the complicated movements required of a jumping horse.

Like ice-skaters who practice tricky leaps, a horse must perfect its moves over and over again, with the precision of clockwork. One jump is not much of a feat. A course of twelve or sixteen jumps of varying sizes and shapes is like an ice-skater's long program. Even with all the practice in the world, the horse still may not succeed each and every time.

With all the knowledge Harry had of horses, he now had a puzzle on his hands—and that is what he liked best. A horse with sufficient spring to jump out of a paddock should be able to carry a rider over a small fence. But Harry had already tried the most rudimentary step for a jumper, and the horse had tripped and stumbled. The gelding was willing, honest, and kind. What he seemed to lack was *ability*. Still, Harry was convinced that Snowman had *some* ability. He was determined to find out.

The first step in training a horse to jump is to teach him to negotiate a series of poles laid on the ground, called *cavaletti*. The poles are spaced six feet apart for a trot, or nine feet apart for a canter. These exercises teach the horse to pace himself and to pick up his feet. In order to trot through the poles without rapping them, a horse must learn to lift his feet higher than usual. Muscle, balance, and good training are all important, just as for human athletes.

At first, an average horse stumbles, unsure about how to time his stride to avoid knocking into the poles. With patience and repetition, however, most horses will learn how to trot over the series of poles without knocking into them. At this point, the horse understands the principle of adjusting his stride to avoid hitting an obstacle. This is the first step. Not every horse masters it right away.

Harry set up poles, evenly spaced on the ground, and headed Snowman toward them at a brisk trot. Snowman tripped, then stumbled, tripped again, then righted himself. Harry patted the horse, dismounted, reset the poles, and tried again.

Once a horse can trot through a series of poles on the ground, the next step is to add a raised pole at the end of the line. Not too high, though; around six inches to start. Most horses will make a small hop over this obstacle. Others might trot over the bar, knocking it over, or refuse to jump it, ducking past it. To take a small hop shows big progress in a horse. It shows that the horse trusts his rider enough to hurl himself airborne and carry his rider with him.

One of the hardest things for a young horse—or a horse like Snowman, who had never jumped with a rider on his back—is to learn how to balance with a rider aboard. After all, a rider of over one hundred pounds changes the horse's natural center of balance. A skilled rider may change it less—but every rider has some effect.

As the horse gains in proficiency, the final pole is raised. Then *two* jumps begin to follow the ground poles. This is known as gymnastic jumping. As the horse practices, he learns how to control the length of his strides. And he learns to gather himself at just the right moment: the moment to take off flying.

Like a ballet dancer, a horse show jumper's abilities are honed to a level of control, skill, and grace that require serious training. What makes the sport of riding so unpredictable and endlessly alluring is that it requires a partnership. With a skilled and sensitive rider aboard, a horse begins to trust in his own abilities. Just as the most brilliant rider is nothing without a great horse, so the greatest horse cannot shine without an equally talented rider.

The equestrian arts have a written history dating back to the Greeks. Styles of riding have evolved over the years. Federico Caprilli, the nineteenth-century chief riding instructor of the Italian cavalry, discovered that if a rider kept his weight forward over a fence, staying with the horse's center of gravity, the rider would be more secure. Then the horse could jump better. Soon enough, this forward position swept across Europe and the United States. With the change in the rider's seat, horses could consistently clear high fences, paving the way for the development of the sport of show jumping.

By the mid-twentieth century, even self-taught riders had adopted the forward seat. But unlike the classically trained U.S. cavalry riders, the style of self-taught professionals was often a little quirky.

A classically trained rider will keep his lower leg mostly perpendicular over a fence, his back straight, and his eyes looking forward. His hands will release forward, giving the horse room to stretch out his neck.

A self-taught rider may achieve the same effect but without the same style, hurling his weight forward over the big jumps, his back rounded. Or he may duck down over the horse's neck, letting his lower legs slide out behind him.

Harry's riding style was a hybrid of these two. He did not have the military training that had influenced many top American riders, but his style was less eccentric than those of some of the other self-taught riders. His balance over the fences was impeccable, allowing him to stay with the horse's motion even over big obstacles.

Harry reset the poles and circled back again, approaching the *cavaletti* at a brisk trot. Again, Snowman stumbled, scattering the poles. But Harry soldiered on, determined to find the key to unlock this horse's ability.

Approaching a jump, a rider must *believe*. The rider must go forward in unison with the horse. Riders who are just learning to jump will often lag a split second behind the horse, waiting in the saddle to make sure the horse takes off. These beginners often fall off as the horse lands. But a skilled rider always goes *with* the horse, giving the power to the horse.

Snowman did not stop at the raised bar. But he did not jump, either. Rather than make a small hop, Snowy broke to a trot over the low cross-rail, not even bothering to pick up his feet. A hind leg rapped the bar with a crisp *thwock*. A moment later, the horse settled down to a walk. Harry laughed, urged the horse into a canter, circled around, and tried again—but this time, the result was even worse. Snowman trotted over the low fence, knocking the pole clean off the standard.

So the first attempt at jumping the horse was unspectacular. But Harry could still picture the solid paddock rail fences that the horse had cleared on his own.

Day after day, in the small paddock behind their farm, Harry took Snowy out and schooled him. After a while, the gelding could trot through the cavaletti poles on the ground, and even mastered a low jump at the end. To give the horse a break, Harry put the kids up on his back, or they rode him to the beach. The horse was good and he was honest—he was still just a little clumsy with his feet.

The summer drew to a close. It was time for Snowman to return to his box stall at the Knox School. But if Harry thought that any of the girls would be happy to see him back, he was wrong. The girls still thought this horse was beneath them. He was placid and kind enough for the beginners, but when Harry suggested riding him over a small fence, the girls would arch their eyebrows. *Snowman? The girls preferred to ride the more graceful, elegant horses instead.*

The fall semester wore on. Ever optimistic, Harry continued to school Snowman over low fences himself, hoping the horse would progress enough to carry the girls over a course of jumps.

Snowy was starting to clear low hurdles without difficulty, but a good jumper snaps his knees up over the fence, raising them almost up to his neck. Snowman did not snap up his knees. He left his forelegs hanging down, and his hooves tended to knock the fences as he went over. It wasn't dangerous, but it it was a bad quality for a show jumper. In a competition, a show jumper horse would lose points for touching *any* part of the fence.

Harry wanted to take Snowy's skills to the next level. So he put his gutsiest rider, Bonnie Cornelius, in the saddle. Normally, he paired her with the most challenging horses, Chief Sunset or Wayward Wind. But Harry wanted to watch Snowman jumping from the ground. Studying a horse's form over fences was important. Maybe watching him with someone else in the saddle would help Harry figure out a better approach.

By the end of the lesson, poles had gone flying every which way. Harry saw the frustration on his talented student's face. If his best rider could not make this horse jump, was there any hope that Snowman would ever jump high over fences?

If Snowman could jump over the rows of pasture fences between his stable and the doctor's house, he must have talent. Then again, if he did have talent, he sure was keeping it well hidden.

Still, Harry kept riding the gelding. One day, he set the jumps up to four feet. He'd been riding Wayward Wind over the fences, and was planning to dismount and lower the poles for Snowy.

Then again, Harry thought, Snowman had been coming along a little—without much trouble, he could clear a three-foot fence, the height of a beginner course. Why not try a bigger jump? What was the worst that could happen? If the fence was too big, the horse would knock it down.

Harry mounted Snowman. As they came around the turn, Harry shifted his weight slightly. With the pressure of his hands on the reins, and a slight squeeze of his leg against the horse's barrel, he headed the big horse toward the jump.

Suddenly, Harry sensed a subtle shift. The horse pricked his ears forward. Electricity pulsed up through the saddle. With a practiced eye, Harry saw the distance to the fence. He lowered his weight slightly, telling the horse to shorten his stride. The horse followed suit, for one stride, two, and . . . Snowman's hindquarters gathered underneath him.

His hocks sank down.

Harry kept the reins loose and his balance forward.

Up and over the fence they flew, front legs well clear of the poles.

Harry listened for the hollow thump of the horse's hind legs trailing over the rail. But there was none. Harry glanced behind him at the big fence they had just cleared, then threw the reins down. Grinning, he patted the horse with both hands. Snowman, relaxed as ever, slowed to a walk.

Snowman could jump after all! Just give him a fence that was high enough. Harry signaled to the horse with a cluck and a nudge. One of Snowman's ears flicked back—a sign that he was listening. He picked up the pace. Harry guided him toward the fence a second time.

Again, in a perfect sequence of movement, the horse sailed over with room to spare.

Flight.

The horse who jumps well jumps for the joy of flight; the rider he brings along with him receives a bountiful gift.

A horse's *scope* refers to its ability to jump high fences. Most horses clear three feet easily. Some horses are comfortable at four or four and a half feet. By the time fences are raised *above* five feet, though, even the better jumpers are starting to reach their limit. Only a few horses are successful at six feet, and heights above seven feet are achieved only by a select group of elite athletes. While some horses can clear obstacles higher than seven feet, the likelihood of a crash is high—and the consequences of crashing from a height of seven feet can be shattering for both horse *and* rider.

Over a five-foot obstacle Snowman flew, snapping up his knees tightly. Next, Harry raised the fences to six feet. Snowman cleared that height with no problem, again snapping his knees tight and reaching forward with his neck to create a higher arc. Harry brought the poles up again, until they were about six feet, six inches. Snowman continued to soar, as if he'd been born with invisible wings.

Each time the horse cleared another high obstacle, it left Harry breathless, sensing the coiled power in this horse. That power had been so well hidden—and now, suddenly, it was unleashed. Harry could not shake the image of the horse running home to him, across meadows and over pasture fences. He remembered Snowman looking at him as if to say, "Here I am."

How many times had someone told Harry about his special gift for horses, his gift for intuition, for speaking to horses in their own language? This time, the horse had stood right in front of him, calling out his message loud and clear—but Harry had not heard it.

If there was one thing Harry himself could not bear, it was to be underestimated, to be judged for something other than his true ability and the content of his character. And now, here before him, was a horse that would gather up and soar over fences so high that he could not see to the other side. For Harry, it was a humbling moment. He was proud of his ability to judge horseflesh, but this time he had been dead wrong. His gentle plow horse had the heart of a lion.

How many years had Harry been looking for just one horse who might have the makings of a champion?

Sometimes a man can forget the most important lesson of all: big dreams are often best accomplished when you do what you can with the materials you have at hand. This eighty-dollar gelding, this lesson horse, this shaggy-coated, friendly, children-loving animal, had hidden his gifts under the plainest, most humble exterior. As Harry himself later repeated, many times over, "I was foolish enough to sell the horse, but the horse, he knew better." He knew well enough to jump paddock fences to find his way home.

CHAPTER 10

THE HORSE BUSINESS

ST. JAMES, LONG ISLAND, SUMMER AND FALL 1957

To many wealthy families in the mid-1950s, horseback riding was a sport that symbolized English, upper-class elegance. Up-and-coming Americans who wanted to enter the exclusive enclaves of the wealthy liked to associate themselves with the glamorous world of horses.

The Knox parents were eager for their girls to have these advantages. They came out to the school on the train from the city. The women were clad in furs. The fathers were all the same—these were men who had money and demanded the best for their girls. Part of Harry's job was finding horses that would make the Knox girls look good at the local horse shows. If a horse joined the lesson lineup and a girl fell in love with it, then later, Harry might be able to sell the horse to her family. If he found a good prospect that was too difficult for a girl to ride, a parent might pay for the horse and hand it over to Harry to train, hoping it would settle down enough to be a suitable junior mount.

Busy as he was with teaching, Harry hadn't let go of his dream of competing in horse shows.

Without enough money to buy himself a horse, Harry's best bet was to find a good prospect for one of his students—a student whose father would put up the cash. Harry could train the horse for a year or two before passing it to the girl to ride, devoting a couple of years to a decent animal, and hopefully winning his share of ribbons. But that horse would not be Harry's *own* horse; it would belong to someone else. Still, that was the fastest way to get into competition—the pathway taken by other professional riders.

Harry had a pretty good prospect in the barn right now: Sinjon. The horse was too challenging for the students to ride, but Harry had started him out himself in some smaller shows. He and Sinjon had even brought home some blue ribbons already.

Sinjon was a Thoroughbred. Right away, the gelding showed talent as a jumper, but he had some flaws. He was a "dirty stopper"—sometimes skidding to a stop right in front of a fence, a dangerous habit that could unseat even the most skilled rider. Not only that, he was so high-strung that he could not relax, even when standing in his stall. All day, he rocked back and forth.

One of the fathers at Knox had noticed Sinjon. He'd agreed to let Harry train the horse and take him to some shows, in the hope that his daughter would eventually ride him.

Sinjon was the dead opposite of Snowman. Where the gray plow horse was placid and easygoing, Sinjon reflected every inch of his thoroughbred breeding. Even though he had been too slow to race successfully, he still had the volatile reflexes and touchy disposition that is bred into Thoroughbreds to make them fast.

When Harry could get Sinjon to keep it together, the gelding did pretty well, and he was a typically handsome Thoroughbred—the kind of horse that looked as if he belonged in the show ring, not as if he used to work the fields.

Horse shows have different divisions, based on the different kinds of work that horses traditionally did. For instance, a "working hunter" galloped and jumped over terrain while engaged in the sport of foxhunting. In the show ring, working hunters are judged on their skill, beauty, and style over fences. In Harry's day, this hunter division was very prestigious—a place where well-heeled amateurs competed on the finest horses money could buy. Fences were of moderate height, and style—expensive, custom-made riding gear, French saddles, and fine English leather bridles—counted in the judging.

At several shows in the spring of 1957, Harry and Sinjon won the "green" hunter division. The green competitions were for horses competing for the first time. Unlike Sinjon, a horse like Snowman could *never* have competed in the hunter division. If he ever made it to a show, Snowman would need to enter in the *jumper division*. This division, where the jumps were the highest and the courses the most complicated, was the only part of a horse show that was judged on skill alone. If a horse cleared a jump, he got points. If he knocked down a fence or refused to jump, he lost points. Open jumpers were not judged on looks, or style, or breeding—only on accomplishment.

Harry much preferred these open jumper contests. Few

amateurs competed in open jumpers. The courses were just too high and too tough. And the stakes were high, too—a spill over a fence, in those days when protective headgear or helmets were not yet worn, could cause catastrophic injury. To Harry, the hunter division just did not carry the same thrill as the jumpers: too much emphasis on looks and style, not enough emphasis on pure adrenaline-rushing performance.

Meanwhile, Harry kept working on Snowman, patiently teaching him to jump, one skill at a time. Although Snowman, the old paddock jumper, handled high fences with ease, he had more trouble jumping not just high but also *wide*. Harry practiced gymnastic jumping with the horse, patiently adding height, then depth to the fences, teaching him to stretch out over a fence when needed.

Growing up on a farm had forever shaped Harry's view of horses. In the world he'd been born into, people and horses spent time on hard physical labor. For Harry, riding was much more than performing in a show ring. Endless hours of mucking and currying, doctoring and schooling went along with it. And horses had their work to do, too.

Snowman's job was to be a dependable lesson horse, and that was what he did, faithfully carrying the girls around on his back. The morning training sessions, the painstaking lessons where the former plow horse had to learn everything from scratch—those were simply added on to the horse's daily routine.

But Harry approached the training of the unglamorous lesson horse with the same care, attention, and dedication that he gave to the more obvious prospects like Sinjon. A lot more training and testing would be needed to see if Snowman *really* had what it took to succeed in competition. Maybe, Harry kept thinking, this horse had a shot.

Deep within Harry burned one desire: he wanted to ride his *own* horse, a horse he had trained with his own hands, nurtured and fed and cared for—not as a hired hand but as part of a team. Snowman was not the most beautiful, not the most naturally talented. Snowman had only one advantage: he—unlike Sinjon—belonged to Harry. Against all odds, Harry was rooting for him.

CHAPTER 11

SNOWMAN'S FIRST SHOW

HUNTINGTON, LONG ISLAND, 1957

By fall 1957, Harry was prepared to take Snowman to his first show. September 5 was the first day of the North Shore Horse Show at the Old Field Club. This was one of the majors. Many top horses from all over would be there, gearing up for the autumn season.

September 5 dawned cool and gray, with a forecast for sunshine later in the day. With his German shepherd Smoky at his heels, Harry headed out to his barn. As usual, he loved the dark, quiet atmosphere of early morning. With the wheelbarrow and pitchfork, he made quick work of the stalls.

Like every other morning, Snowy was the first to hang his head over the Dutch door, giving three loud whinnies when he heard Harry's footsteps. Even in the dim light, the gelding's coat glowed from all the extra grooming, and the braided forelock showed off his small ears. While he still wasn't much of a looker, he cleaned up nice.

One of Harry's summer students, Louie Jongacker, got to

the barn early. The boy greeted Harry, carrying his polished boots and hunt coat. Cast-off horses were not the only thing that seemed to show up at Hollandia. Teenage boys collected around Harry's farm just like stray dogs. Johanna always seemed able to set another place at the table, and Harry could always find something for a spare boy to do—driving the tractor, helping out with the horses.

New students with money to spend on lessons and horses were good for business, but a kid did not need money to be able to ride at Hollandia Farms. When a new teenager, like Louie, showed up shyly offering to work in exchange for lessons, Harry always found a way to take them in. In the snooty town that surrounded St. James, the de Leyer household was a place where everyone felt equally valued. All a young man or woman needed to survive there was a capacity for hard work. For a number of them, experiencing the force of Harry's personality and Johanna's gentle dignity were key formative experiences in their young lives.

The de Leyers didn't ask a lot of questions. There was enough work on the farm to keep kids out of trouble. Life wasn't easy in St. James for kids from the wrong side of the tracks. The de Leyers, as young new immigrants, were welcoming of all. Harry and Johanna both radiated strength of character. They didn't care what your last name was or what estate you came from but respected what you made of yourself.

Harry was taking Louie Jongacker along to the show. Louie was from Queens, but in the summer, he helped with barn chores at Harry's farm. A tall, skinny lad, he was not a natural in the saddle. But the boy was a hard worker, and Harry wanted to give him a taste of riding in a competition. Over the summer,

Snowman had been coming along well. He'd been trained to the point where he could negotiate the turns and pacing of a simple jumping course. Since Harry needed a mount for Louie, he decided to let him give Snowman a try.

Harry trusted Snowman to give Louie a safe ride. The gelding did not always have the precision to avoid hitting fences, but he was an honest horse—he never refused a jump. The boy would experience the thrill of riding in front of a crowd. And Snowy would enjoy it, too. He did not have to earn a ribbon; just being here, healthy and clean, braided up like a prize-winning horse, was a triumph in itself.

The North Shore show spanned three days. Upon arrival, competitors, trainers, and grooms all scurried around, stabling their horses. In the barn, pampered riders leaned back on camp chairs while grooms blacked their tall, custom-made boots. Everyone's nerves were on edge.

Harry smiled as Snowman sauntered down the ramp toward the barn. The gelding looked around the showgrounds calmly, as if he'd been doing this all his life.

Junior jumpers, Snowman's first class, was the last junior class of the day.

Harry had butterflies in his stomach when young Louie swung into the saddle and settled on Snowman's broad back. The boy looked nervous and a little stiff. He was eager, but afraid. "Take it easy," Harry called out. "Just ride like you always do."

The schooling ring, where horses warmed up before the

show ring, was crowded with riders. Trainers yelled commands to the boys and girls on horseback. Nervous parents lined up along the fence.

Harry didn't say much—he just watched.

He adjusted the bars on one of the practice fences, then nodded. Louie circled around toward the jump. When Snowman cleared the fence easily, Louie's body loosened up a little.

Next, Harry raised the poles to about four feet. He nodded at Louie. "Once more."

The boy's eyes widened, but he didn't protest. He just circled around to take the fence one more time.

"Don't flap your wings like a chicken!" Harry called, signaling the boy to tuck his elbows in closer to his sides. He could see Louie's hands stiffening up nervously, throwing the big horse just slightly off his stride. But then Snowman gathered up. The big horse cleared the fence with room to spare. Louie's face broke into a huge grin. Harry smiled, too.

Snowman didn't go until late in the lineup. The course was not difficult—a simple round of eight fences, each set to three and a half feet. So far, only one horse had gone clean, without touching the fences. When the gray entered the ring, Harry held his breath. He couldn't bear for the horse or his young rider to be a laughingstock.

Steady and sure, the horse circled the course, ears pointed forward, as though this were just another day at Knox. With each fence, he gathered, tucked up his knees, and jumped.

At the end of the round, Snowman had no faults. When the class finished, he had the only clean round. The tall, skinny boy from Queens trotted out of the ring with Snowman, carrying a blue ribbon. A huge grin shone on Louie's face. Harry stood at the in-gate, beaming as wide as if Louie were one of his own children.

Finally, it was time for Harry to get on board Snowman. Harry had entered his horse in the two green jumper classes. Now, Snowman was going to face fences higher than he was used to. He did not expect a ribbon. His goal was simple: to make it around the course without being eliminated—and to show that Snowman was more than a paddock jumper.

Harry circled around, flew over one big fence twice, then slowed to a walk. No point in tiring the horse out with too many practice jumps. After a few minutes, he sat astride Snowman near the railing to watch the other horses. A couple of the top riders put in clean rounds, with no faults. Harry was impressed.

When it was Harry's turn, he headed into the ring at a walk. People in the crowd laughed into their hands and gave each other looks. Was this guy really entering the class riding a school horse?

Despite having been groomed and braided, Snowman stuck out from the fancy horses. Harry knew that he and his mount looked out of place. The horses competing in this green jumper class represented some of the country's top prospects. Some might even reach the international ranks.

Gathering up his reins, Harry cued the horse with a slight nudge of his lower left leg. Snowman lumbered along at a docile canter, his nose stretched out just the way it was when they went on country rides. Harry squeezed his calves around the horse's barrel, and Snowman lengthened his stride without missing a beat. He was paying attention. Harry kept his eyes forward, his weight balanced, and his reins slightly slack.

On this, the horse's first real horse-show challenge, Harry needed his mount to know that he believed. Through the reins, through his seat, through the gentle pressure of his calves on the horse's sides, Harry telegraphed a message: *You can do this.* Snowman pricked his ears forward, gathered his haunches underneath him, and flew. One fence accomplished, and Harry headed him toward the next obstacle with a steady hand. The first few fences, the horse jumped clean. Over the oxer—a kind of wide jump with two rails—he brushed one of the top rails for two faults. This pushed him out of the running for a ribbon.

On the way out of the ring, Harry threw down the reins and gave his horse a big pat. Only two faults. A solid performance for the first time out.

Outside the ring, Harry saw two riders, Dave Kelley and Al Fiore. They were sitting side by side, both grinning as if they owned the world. Fiore had a right to look cocky: he had been the leading point winner on the circuit for the past two years running. He was tall and broad-shouldered, over six feet tall, and a good fifty pounds heavier than Harry. A self-taught horseman, the son of a livery stable owner in Queens, he was a crowd pleaser—his acrobatic style in the saddle made the crowds grip the edges of their seats. Al and Dave shared a laugh as they stared at Harry's flea-bitten gray. Neither of them would have been caught dead riding an old lesson horse into the ring in a top-rated show. This upstart on a plow horse was no competition for their big Thoroughbreds.

Let 'em laugh, Harry thought. Just a few short months ago, he had been walking behind the horse on a long line, teaching him how to steer. Now this horse could make a creditable performance in a jumper class. He may not have gone clean, but he had tried his best. There were several more classes. Maybe they were laughing too soon.

The next class in the green jumper division was the *knock-down-and-out class*. In knock-down-and-out classes, touches would not count as a fault. Only knocking down poles would. Because of this, the fences were much higher, and horses were timed for speed.

Al Fiore's mount, Riviera Topper, was up first. Fiore expertly guided the horse around the course. His flashy moves in the saddle made the course look difficult, but Harry saw that the horse had no trouble with the fences. Several more horses went, each knocking down at least one pole. When it was time to get on Snowman, Harry swung up. This course was more difficult than the previous one. He wasn't sure how Snowy would respond to the challenge.

Waiting at the in-gate, the horse stood half-asleep, his ears flopping at angles, looking every inch the lesson horse. When the gate swung open, Harry gathered his reins and urged Snowman into a trot. Few spectators were even watching. Harry had Snowman canter a tight circle, then headed for the first fence. That's when he felt a sudden click of engagement. *Now, Snowman was paying attention.* As Snowy gathered his hindquarters to take off for the first jump, Harry sensed the raw power coiled within him.

When they trotted out of the ring at the end of the round, they had gone clean. Harry looked over at Al and Dave; they were still laughing. One clean round was nothing—any horse could have *one* good round. Winning required doing it again and again.

The hurdles were raised for the deciding round, or jump-off. Harry felt a small flutter of excitement. Now it was getting interesting. Snowman usually did better when the fences were higher. But he had never faced a course this big in competition.

Snowman sailed over the first fence with room to spare. Next up was an oxer fence. Up and over Snowy went—but he knocked down a pole. As he crossed the last fence, another pole fell. Al Fiore's mount, Riviera Topper, won the class easily. Snowman's jump-off performance was good enough for third place. The rookie plow horse was already in the top three! Snowy proudly trotted back into the ring to pick up the yellow ribbon. When Harry came out, he handed the ribbon to his children for safekeeping. They squealed in delight.

Back at the stables, Harry rubbed Snowy down with liniment and scratched his neck, chuckling when the horse curled his lip into a smile. Snowman's ribbons were hung proudly in the van.

With Snowman settled, Harry returned to the arena and leaned against the fence to watch the open jumpers. It was the final event of the day. Crowds were pressed up against the fences, packing the bleachers. The fences had been raised up to four and a half feet—as a starting point. The poles would get even higher in the jump-offs.

When Riviera Wonder, the reigning national champion, came into the ring with Al Fiore aboard, Harry snapped to attention. Like Snowman, the horse was gray, but the resemblance ended there. A Thoroughbred gelding, he came from a distinguished line of show jumpers. His full sister was already an

Olympic show jumper. Riviera Wonder, Harry saw, had pretty much everything: style, grace, athleticism, and heart. Al Fiore and Riviera Wonder were two-time national jumper champions. With the big show at Madison Square Garden just three months away, they were the hands-down favorite to win again.

Al Fiore's style over a jumper course was strong but unusual—at the fences, he threw himself forward, leaning so far over the horse's neck that he appeared to almost click up his heels behind him. It made the crowds gape with surprise.

Harry watched quietly. He respected Fiore as a rider, but that crazy sudden motion he made with his upper body over fences would throw many horses off balance.

Only one horse in this class could compete with Riviera Wonder, and that was Dave Kelley's mare, Andante. After the first round, everyone had been eliminated but these two. The jump crew worked fast, raising the fences for the second round. Now the smallest obstacle was over five feet tall.

Riviera Wonder came up first. Fiore was a rough rider, but his years of experience showed. He guided the horse around the course with panache. Each time he seemed to click his heels behind him over the fence, the crowd gasped audibly. Each time, the horse landed with a thump, leaving the bars intact. Another clean round.

Next up was Dave Kelley on Andante. An incredibly competitive rider, Dave had more championships under his belt than even Al Fiore. Harry recognized the particular quality that drove Dave. He won a lot because he was so good, but he wasn't in it just to win. He was in it for the love of the game.

Where Al had made the course look challenging, Dave made it look easy. But on the last fence, Andante got a little sloppy with a hind leg. She rubbed the rail and sent flying the light piece of balsa wood that sat atop it. One half fault for a rear touch.

Riviera Wonder was the winner.

If he ever hoped to move up to the open jumper division, this was the level of performance Harry would have to compete against. In the open jumpers, there were no lesson horses, no former plow horses who'd just recently learned to jump. Just champion horses and tough-as-nails riders who had been competing for years.

In the green jumper stakes, Snowman had placed sixth. But this was a horse with almost no training. Even thinking about trying to train Snowman to compete against horses like Riviera Wonder and Andante, some of the country's best jumpers, seemed like a crazy gamble. Harry would have to devote many more hours to training—while also managing all of his other duties. Teaching, tending to the barn, being with his family.

After the show, Harry loaded up the van and headed out for hamburgers with his kids. Maybe nobody knew who he was. Maybe people wanted to laugh at him for riding an old plow horse. But he had ribbons on the dashboard of the truck to bring home tonight. These ribbons belonged to him, to his family, to Snowman, and to Hollandia Farms. Not the ribbons he had been winning for other people, like Sinjon's owner.

From where he and Snowman had started out, those ribbons represented a huge accomplishment.

After the North Shore Horse Show, a desire lodged deep inside Harry and would not let go. He'd felt such pride upon hearing the announcement over the loudspeaker: "Snowman, owned by Mr. and Mrs. Harry de Leyer, ridden by Harry de Leyer." Sometimes it seemed to Harry that for a man in the horse business, his desire to be his own man worked against him. Harry wanted his own champion. Not a horse that would be sold away from him, or that he would train for someone *else's* glory.

Back in Holland, especially during the war, Harry's family had faced extreme scarcity. They had been forced to make do with what they had. By comparison, his life in the United States was one of abundance. He remembered the war years when the de Leyers had cut corners to keep the farm going. If you want something badly enough, Harry always believed, you have to work with the materials you have.

So much of Harry's worldview was shaped by World War II. Just closing his eyes, he could still remember the day during the war when the thatched straw roof of the small Catholic hospital in St. Oedenrode caught on fire. He, along with many of the other young men of the village, were members of the volunteer fire department. They assembled close enough to see the flames, but there was gunfire coming from both directions. The much-needed fire hose lay behind enemy lines. The men decided to draw straws to see who would go.

Harry looked around that circle of men, their eyes barely illuminated in the dark. He knew each one of them, had gone to school with them, worked alongside them, seen them courting their girls at carnivals, and sat next to them in the pews at church, their heads bowed. Harry was the youngest, and the only one who had no wife or children yet.

Before giving it a thought, he volunteered to do it. His father said, "You don't have to go, son," but he made no move to stop him. He was a quiet man, but Harry knew he was proud.

Crawling on his hands and knees down the alleyway toward the hospital, Harry could hear the *pock-pock* of gunfire. He was too concentrated on his task to think about the danger. When dawn brightened the sky, the hospital was still standing, and the American and British troops had driven the Nazis out of St. Oedenrode. After the war, Harry was surprised to receive a plaque for his bravery. He did not think what he'd done was brave—it was a job that needed doing, and he had done it.

Some horses were like that, too, Harry thought—born with a strong, steely will to do what needs to be done. Just like Snowman.

That fall, life was as busy as ever. The family was still growing, with five children now. Every morning, Johanna put breakfast on the table, the family gathered to say grace, and after the meal, everyone set to work. The older boys were able to help out in the barn. Harriet handled some of the grooming. As soon as a child was old enough, they were given a job to do.

It was a good life, more than Harry might have expected, enough that he knew he should be grateful for what he had. Look what he and Johanna had built in just seven short years: a steady job, a growing family, a home of their own. They had worked hard and they had been lucky. Harry could look around and see that, where he was, he could probably settle down for a long time, teaching the girls and then saying goodbye to them, watching his children grow, giving lessons in the summertime.

Perhaps Harry and Snowman hadn't made much of an impression at the North Shore show. Especially among all of the already-famous riders. But Harry kept thinking about that third-place ribbon in the knock-down-and-out class.

Harry knew what he saw in Snowman, that special quality that nobody else had noticed. Snowy had a gift. No matter where it came from, it was a gift that no one could take away.

Sure, it was a good life, but Harry was only twenty-nine years old. He was far from ready to settle down. He couldn't help imagining himself climbing aboard his plow horse and the two of them soaring together—buoyed along by the desire to fly.

CHAPTER 12

SINJON

ST. JAMES, LONG ISLAND, 1957

Champion racehorses like Man o' War, Seabiscuit, and Secretariat all come from bloodlines that for generations have been bred for one goal: speed. But speed doesn't necessarily make a horse good at *jumping*. The dazzling, magical quality that separates a good jumper from a great one is hard to pinpoint. Most horses can jump. Some can jump high. But only a very few have the courage, trust, and stamina to carry a rider over a course designed to test those very qualities.

The summer of 1957 had been a good season for Harry. He had won a few ribbons, even though people still sometimes stared at him as though he had stumbled into their party without an invitation.

Among the horses in Harry's barn, there was Wayward Wind, the beautiful chestnut mare. She was a good jumper, but she lacked a certain spark. There was also Night Arrest, a filly that belonged to one of his students. She was a talented handful—but she was hard to ride.

Of course, there was Snowman, the implausible paddock jumper. Of all the horses in the barn, Snowman was the least likely prospect. He had scope, and personality in spades—but he was clumsy. Harry planned to keep training him; maybe he could improve by spring.

And then there was Sinjon. The jumpy Thoroughbred seemed like the best prospect to become a jumper champion. He had lost his scrawny look and had filled out nicely.

Harry had a winning summer season with Sinjon, leading in points for the green hunter championship. But at Sands Point, the week after North Shore, a judge pulled Harry aside. He told Harry that Sinjon held his head too high, and didn't have the right manner to be a champion in the hunter division. After all, in the hunter division, judging was based on a horse's looks as well as a good performance.

Harry felt sure that this touchy, erratic, hot-blooded horse had talent—and he wanted to give Sinjon a chance to prove himself. Maybe Sinjon could compete in the jumper division instead of the hunter division. He was an excellent jumper with lots of spring, and in these classes, no one would look at the way he carried his head. Only the ability to clear the fences would count.

But the short, fall show season was nearly over now. The only horse shows left on the calendar were the top-flight competitions on the indoor circuit. The crown jewel was the National Horse Show at Madison Square Garden.

Harry pitched the idea to Sinjon's owner, Mr. Dineen, the father of one of his students at Knox. What if he tried out Sinjon at the National? It was a crazy idea. The National Horse Show was *the* top horse show in the country. The horse had never competed in a jumper class, so Harry would have to enter in the rounds that were open to beginners. Sinjon would be in front of a glittering crowd that numbered in the tens of thousands.

Maybe Mr. Dineen liked the young horseman's outsized confidence. Slowly, he nodded yes. Harry couldn't get a whole week off from work, but he got permission to take Sinjon to the National to compete for a few days.

Nothing ventured, nothing gained. Entry was a long shot—not likely to lead to anything. Mr. Dineen and his daughter Eileen would be up in the stands watching. Harry vowed to do his best and make Sinjon's owner think the trip had been worthwhile.

The seventy-fourth annual National Horse Show at Madison Square Garden opened on November 5, 1957, with its usual fanfare. The show brought together the top equine competitors from all over the country—and the whole world.

Crews worked furiously, putting the last touches on the basement stables. Ten to twelve inches of dirt were layered over the steel platform floor. Decorations and flags of all the represented nations were hung from the balustrade. The National Horse Show social rituals, on pause during World War II, were now back in full swing. The boxes in the "golden circle" around the show ring were full of wealthy notables and socialites, some whose families had been part of the tradition since 1883. During the eight-day course of the show at Madison Square Garden, the spectacle of rich people in their finery was as much a draw as the horses.

The show's opening ceremony would even be broadcast live on television—a big deal at the time. There was something for every kind of horse fan, for roadsters and pleasure horses, saddle horses and walkers. But nothing riled up the crowd as much as the thrills and spills of the open jumper competitions. Whichever horse won the open jumper division was acknowledged to be the top jumper in the show—and the top horse in the nation.

This year, Riviera Wonder was the hands-down favorite for that title, expected to repeat his performances of '55 and '56. Eleonora Sears's gelding Diamant, who'd even been in the Olympics, was considered a close second. Dave Kelley's mare Andante was also a strong contender.

For Harry de Leyer, this impressive show was a chance to try out Sinjon against the best. Any horse could enter the class—but few had the skills to try.

The courses were challenging and the fences were high— a horse jumping over a five- or six-foot fence catapults a rider more than ten feet into the air. Riders wore no protective gear, and spectacular crashes happened frequently in this high-risk, high-stakes game. One wrong move over a fence that size could cause a catastrophic crash. Sometimes a rider or a horse fell so hard that he or she would never walk away.

The qualifying classes took place on weekday mornings, when the crowds were sparse. The top twelve from all those rounds would get to ride during the evening performances. That's when the big crowds really showed up. The most popular classes, the open jumper classes, often ran late into the night. Jump-offs sometimes lasted until one or two o'clock in the morning.

Harry didn't expect to make it out of morning elimination. In the first class, Sinjon, spooked by the strange sounds and smells at the Garden, put in a lackluster performance. He didn't make it into the evening round. That night, Harry sat in the stands, high up in the cheap seats, and watched the chosen warriors battle it out. With his trained eye, he carefully sized up the competition.

For a moment, Harry imagined that he was under the spotlights, riding Snowman. The thought made him smile. The big plow horse probably wouldn't mind the lights and the crowds, but Harry could practically hear the hoots of laughter that would greet their entry to the ring.

These horses at Madison Square Garden were seasoned competitors—all sleek and beautiful, all bred to be equine athletes. Snowman probably couldn't measure up against these horses yet, but Harry believed that Sinjon could. The courses at the National were tough, too. Nothing like the ones Sinjon had been competing on over the summer. The fences were high, the ring was small, and the crowds were noisy and distracting.

Harry didn't get caught up in the hoopla of the event. He had a job to do, and that was to ride Sinjon to victory. The life upstairs, where socialites posed for photographers, didn't concern him.

The next day, Sinjon was calmer, more settled. A new class was starting, and Harry had another shot. This time, on his second try, Sinjon completed a clean round. They had qualified for the nighttime class! That night, Harry would be facing off against some of the most seasoned performers on the circuit.

Riding at night in a big indoor show is an experience like no other. The sights, sounds, and smells in the huge arena, under the lights, were completely foreign to Sinjon, a horse from a small, rural barn.

The arena in the Garden was smaller than most. Tight corners left the horses little room to maneuver. A walkway known as the promenade surrounded the ring. The lighting was strange—spotlights from different angles cast unexpected shadows—and the press box was stuffed with photographers, whose flashes popped nonstop. Even the most seasoned horse show competitor, man or beast, felt the pressure.

Upstairs now, in the waiting aisle for the night class, Harry sat astride Sinjon. The horse vibrated like a live wire under Harry's seat. The bay chomped nervously on his bit and flicked his ears back whenever he got close to the other horses.

Sinjon had performed well in the outdoor horse shows. But those had been big, rangy courses, where horses could gallop freely and had plenty of room. Here, in this small, cramped ring, Harry couldn't be sure what his horse would do.

The moment when the announcer calls a horse's name and number, at any show, no matter how small, is the moment when a rider realizes: *This is the moment. The time is now.*

At the 1957 National Horse Show, that moment took place in a noisy, smoke-filled, glaring arena. When the top competitors rode, a hush fell over the crowd; but Harry and Sinjon were unknown, so the low patter of conversation, the crackling of programs, and soft laughter continued unabated.

Harry clasped his calves around Sinjon and lightened his pressure on the reins just slightly, signaling the horse to bound ahead. The horse was contained, but just barely. Sinjon craned his head around, looking at the unfamiliar sights of the night-time arena under the lights—and that was not a good start. Harry nudged Sinjon into a controlled gallop and kept him on a tight rein. He circled around, then headed toward the first fence.

Sinjon took the first two fences cleanly. *Phew!* Harry thought. But then, on the third fence, he heard a *crack* and felt the horse's foreleg drop a pole. Still, for the rest of the course, the horse was clear.

Outside the arena, Harry watched the other competitors work. It was a challenging course. Poles went flying every which way.

At the end of the class, Riviera Wonder was on top with a clear round. He had first place in the bag.

When the judges called the rest of the ribbons, Harry was shocked. Out of the twelve top competitors from the morning round, Harry and Sinjon had earned fourth place—a staggering performance for this unknown rider on his rookie horse!

Harry beamed. Now, at last, he knew that everybody could see what he had been saying all along. This horse, though hard to ride, had the flash and brilliance to compete at the championship level. He just needed a year or two of seasoning. Harry had a real Thoroughbred to train—a horse with the potential to be a champion.

For the rest of the show, when he wasn't riding, Harry watched the fanfare from the stands. It brought back vivid memories of his own few years jumping in Europe. Back then, people had predicted that one day Harry de Leyer would represent Holland in international competitions.

Maybe, he wondered, he would have ridden in the Olympics

himself, if he had never left home. But Harry reminded himself to count his blessings. Here he was, at the National Horse Show. By any definition, it was better than he could have hoped a few short years ago.

From his perch in the stands, Harry admired Bill Steinkraus, the captain of the United States Equestrian Team. Bill was a graceful rider who was as capable as he was elegant. Next, Harry gritted his teeth through the German performances—the war was still fresh in Harry's mind. He watched the pluck and determination of Colonel Humberto Mariles of the Mexican team, a crowd favorite who tore around the courses clad in military garb festooned with gold braid. Mariles had an exuberant style that made him one of a kind.

On the last day, Sinjon's owner, Mr. Dineen, came to find Harry, saying he had fantastic news.

Before hearing another word, Harry was immediately excited. Being at the Garden, seeing the best of the best, he had begun imagining a glorious future with Sinjon. He was already envisioning their return next fall—how well the horse would perform with another year of seasoning under his belt. Maybe Sinjon was the champion he had always dreamed of finding.

But in the course of one short conversation, those hopes were dashed. Mr. Dineen's "fantastic news" wasn't so fantastic for Harry. It turned out that George Morris, a young rider who had competed with the United States Equestrian Team in the 1956 Rome Olympics, had noticed Sinjon. Morris believed the horse could make it in international competition. Mr. Dineen had been asked to loan the horse to the United States Equestrian Team.

With Morris aboard, Sinjon would be trained under the

tutelage of Bertalan de Némethy, the coach of the U.S. Equestrian Team. Sinjon would be given every opportunity to develop his talent, receiving the very best coaching available in the United States.

Harry knew George Morris. He had watched him come up through the juniors—where his precise riding style had helped him win two important junior equestrian championships.

George Morris had talent, and he had opportunity.

Harry de Leyer was not in a position to stand in his way.

With a heavy heart, Harry handed Sinjon's lead rope to a groom for the United States Equestrian Team. He watched Sinjon walk away from him, disappearing into the hands of another rider. Harry knew the horse was good. He probably knew better than anyone what Sinjon was capable of.

Harry walked back to his truck empty-handed. He had no horse to trailer back to Long Island. Just an empty van, rattling along behind him in the cold November night. On the seat next to him lay the white fourth-place ribbon, embossed in bright gold.

Harry's life so far seemed to be trying to teach him a lesson: don't wish for what you don't have. And yet, these past few days had given him just the briefest taste of life under the hot spotlights of big-time riding competition, enough to let him know that he wanted to taste it again. He did not have the money to buy a finely bred horse. Nor was he in a position to keep a horse when the United States Equestrian Team came calling.

Someday, Harry had no doubt, Sinjon would perform in front of European crowds, maybe even in the Olympic games.

His rider would be proud, and rightly so. But when that horse was led back to the barn, the rider would hand his reins to a groom. Harry, on the other hand, wanted to do both. Ride his horses, *and* take care of them. That was not the way things were done, especially among wealthy riders who could hire people to take care of their horses for them.

But Harry had never been one to accept the status quo.

He belonged in that ring, with the men riding the open jumpers. He knew he could do it. A rider, however, is only one part of the equation. A rider must have a horse.

As he rattled east across Long Island, away from the bright lights of the city and toward Suffolk County, he thought about his next step.

Crazy as it might seem, he couldn't help thinking of his quiet lesson horse, Snowman. What if that placid mount—the one that his kids loved, the one who wouldn't hurt a fly—had the makings of a champion? Sure, getting a third-place ribbon in a green jumper class in a local show did not mean much of anything, but Harry felt it deep inside himself. He believed Snowy had untapped potential—unfulfilled promise that mirrored his own.

CHAPTER 13

THE CIRCUIT

SANDS POINT, SUMMER 1958

The horse show season had officially begun. The Seashore Circuit, a series of three Long Island shows, would kick off in June. The first show would be at Sands Point, west of St. James on Long Island's North Shore. And in 1958, Sands Point was a new kind of horse show. It didn't have the stuffy feel of other Long Island horse shows. Instead, the show grounds were packed with children and families out for a weekend spectacle.

This show would be Snowman's first test of the new season. Here was the moment to find out whether all of his winter schooling had paid off. Harry had patiently trained his horse to jump over different kinds of fences. Still, there was no way to predict how he'd handle an unfamiliar course in a new place. The only way to find out was to give it a try.

With Knox closed for the summer, there was nothing to stop Harry—no school events or anxious headmistresses. The summer season of 1958 was all his.

On June 9, Harry rose at four in the morning. The de Leyers

did everything together as a family, and getting ready for a show was no exception. While other trainers worked alongside professional grooms, Harry and Johanna treated the trip to the show as a family outing. Chef and Harriet were up early, too, helping out with the horses, feeding, grooming, loading equipment and horses onto the van.

Sands Point was in Port Washington, about thirty-five miles west along the North Shore. Johanna and the children rode in the station wagon, and Harry drove the van with the horses. When they arrived at the show, the grounds were already bustling with people. A thousand horses had been entered to compete.

Even among the huge crowds, Harry instantly noticed Andante, the big bay Thoroughbred, standing proud in the stables. There was no denying it: that horse looked like royalty. Her stall was tidy and decorated with beautiful, monogrammed drapes. In fact, most of the stalls throughout the stables looked impeccable, with perfectly groomed Thoroughbreds peering out over the Dutch doors.

The stabling area was filled with riders and trainers, all zipping past each other. Several grooms, immaculately turned out in khakis, some sporting driver's caps, tended to the horses— combing out tails until they were silken, polishing hooves with pine tar, or emptying plump grain into scrubbed-out rubber buckets. The de Leyers didn't have money for the kinds of fancy custom-made drapes, hand-painted tack trunks, and embroidered blankets that the other stables used to identify their horses. Each horse wore an oiled leather halter with a polished engraved brass name tag on it. Next to each stall a white lead rope hung, coiled in a perfect loop.

But even the most elegant horses in this show would find it difficult to beat Andante.

Andante's rider, Dave Kelley, was a friendly man and a superb trainer. The two were a stellar combination. An air force veteran who had served in World War II, Dave was liked and admired by everyone. Most horse people considered him to be one of the best professional riders on the East Coast.

Harry had brought four horses with him: his chestnut mare Wayward Wind, a hunter named Cicero, his student's flighty and difficult horse Night Arrest to compete in the green division, and Snowman. Of the four, Snowman looked the *least* likely to be there. While the other horses paced nervously in the new surroundings, Snowman contentedly munched on his hay while the de Leyer children clustered around him—excited that their favorite horse had come to compete in a real horse show.

They were convinced that their Snowy would win.

The show's first events were the hunter classes, where horses are judged on style and performance alone. Next up was the jumper division. Harry would be riding Snowman. Braided and groomed to a shine for his first class, today he looked more like a city slicker than an old plow horse. He'd been carefully clipped and trimmed. His bridle and headgear had been taken apart piece by piece, carefully soaped and buffed to a sheen. Harry slipped a soft rubber snaffle into the horse's mouth. He tucked the horse's ears under the crownpiece one by one, then tightened the throat latch.

Harry was almost finished prepping. He took his blue saddle blanket and folded it four times, laid it carefully on the big gray's back, and then settled his saddle on top.

Now the horse was all ready to go.

Harry could not help but notice the way the spectators re-acted at the sight of him, chuckling to themselves. He could guess what they were thinking. That he was some local yokel with an old farm horse, somebody who'd stumbled into an A-rated show by accident and didn't stand a chance. The amusement—perhaps even scorn—in the air was obvious.

Yet Harry sat astride his flea-bitten gray with the calm of a prince, surveying the ring with his penetrating blue eyes.

The judge was ready with his clipboard. It was time for the first jumper class to start.

The ring's gate swung open. All eyes were on Dave Kelley and his mare Andante. Horse and rider were both veterans, rounding courses with an air of self-assuredness. Harry watched from the sidelines, well aware that Andante had been winning national championships long before Snowman had stumbled over his first pole. The pair set off toward the first fence with an air of assumed victory. And the performance was flawless—almost. Andante rubbed one fence with a hind foot. Any horse with a clean round could beat her. So far, nobody had.

Harry and Snowman waited by the sidelines, watching. Snowman stood still, his ears flopping to the sides, the reins looped loose at the side of his neck as he waited his turn. His manner stood in contrast to the other horses. Most appeared nervous, held in check with tight reins, prancing in place and sometimes chomping at their bits until flecks of foam speckled their cheeks and spotted their chests.

Many of the horses wore complicated leather straps—from standing martingales that tethered the horse's head to a strap around its neck, to draw reins that ran over the horse's poll just behind his ears, through the rings of the bit, and back to the rider's hand, acting as a pulley. Unlike Snowman, with his soft rubber snaffle, those horses were also outfitted with complicated metal bitting whose ferocious names, like "scissor bits" and "double twisted wire," indicated their severity. Their riders had spurs strapped to their heels, and crops—short, stiff whips—in their hands, trying to keep their horses in a narrow tunnel between their two legs and two hands, giving their mounts no corner to duck out to the side of the fence to avoid jumping. On the approach, a rider often appeared to make a series of sharp jerks on the reins, followed by brisk application of the crop. Rider after rider seemed to be forcing the horse around the course. Judging from the other performances, jumping seemed to require a degree of brute force—not cooperation. But this was not Harry's style. As he watched, he stroked the side of Snowman's neck, allowing the gray to relax. He was confident that Snowman would do his best—there was no need for the whips and spurs and other harsh devices that their fellow riders used.

After a few more rounds, the announcer called out Snowman's name. Harry heard a light smattering of applause from the stands.

Right away, the difference was obvious. Snowman looked like a friendly kid entering the playground. He craned his neck around, surveying the crowd, and caught sight of the de Leyer children lined up next to the fence, grinning. Later, the children swore he winked.

Harry cued Snowman to canter. Together, they headed toward the first fence. Unlike the previous riders, who had held their horses on tight reins to keep their heads held high, Harry had a different approach. He let Snowman gallop on a loose rein with his nose outstretched. It was a sign of trust.

Harry, lean and wiry, balanced lightly in his stirrups. As the big horse cleared each jump, Harry was quiet, seeming to expect the horse's movements rather than follow them. The big gray did not appear to be in a hurry. Most of the other horses scattered their energy, chomping and prancing, swinging from side to side, but Snowman loped along steadily, directing all his attention to the task at hand. Harry let the reins slip through his fingers as he felt the horse stretch out his nose the way they had practiced so many times. Harry believed that he needed to allow the horse to find his *own* way—just as he had done so well naturally, jumping paddock fences by himself. As Snowman approached each fence, with his head lowered, his neck extended, and his ears pricked forward, he never showed a moment's hesitation. Up and over.

The next obstacles were chicken coop, oxer, and parallel bars. As they took off over the last oxer fence, Snowman cleared it with room to spare. A clean round.

Harry beamed. He threw down the reins and gave his horse a big, loving pat. There was a pause, and then the entire crowd burst into applause. But this time, it was genuine, not teasing.

When the class was over, the announcer called out the ribbon winners over the PA system, starting with the eighth-place ribbon.

Dave Kelley smiled and waved at the crowd as he went in to receive his red second-place rosette. When the announcer called the winner into the ring, the crowd hooted with joy. Harry jogged into the ring, leading Snowman on a loose rein. Aboard the big horse were three children lined up in order of size: Chef in front, Harriet sandwiched in the middle, and Marty hanging on behind for dear life.

Harry accepted the blue ribbon, then smiled and waved at the crowd. His children waved along with him. He caught sight of Johanna standing in the bleachers, smiling.

This horse show would last three days, but the crowd was already rooting for the plow horse.

CHAPTER 14

THE CINDERELLA HORSE

SANDS POINT, SUMMER 1958

Marie Lafrenz, the head of publicity for the Sands Point show, was up in the bleachers, a manual typewriter balanced on her knees. Marie had grown up in Park Slope, Brooklyn, raised by her grandparents. She took up riding as a girl and was a fearless competitor. Now, Marie covered thirty annual horse shows for the *New York Herald Tribune*. She still loved horses, so she used her writing skills to help drum up excitement for horse shows, in the hopes that they would be picked up by the local papers.

Marie, who knew the New York newspaper business, calculated that if she wrote something interesting about the Sands Point show, she might score coverage in the papers. Horse show publicity might bring in big crowds. And it would help make the sport a mainstream event—drawing in more fans, and helping to give the extraordinary equine athletes their due.

To Marie, it seemed like the more horses disappeared from farms and everyday life, the more iconic they became. By the

1950s, as families moved off farms and into suburbs, signs of nostalgia about horses—TV westerns, horse-themed books and movies—were everywhere. Marie had discovered that some words seemed to carry a special magic. *Olympic rider, ex-racehorse,* and *Thoroughbred* always seemed to get the press's attention. She also liked to come up with a catchphrase or a slogan. As one of the very few woman sports reporters of her day, Marie knew from experience that she needed to try extra hard to carve out a niche for her work.

In 1958, it was clear that television was changing the way people saw spectator sports. Newspapers could not compete with the visual medium of television on its own terms, so they struck at a different angle—not live action, but great stories. Perched in the bleachers at Sands Point, Maria Lafrenz was looking for an attention-grabbing news story.

That's when a big grayish plow horse with a striking young Dutchman aboard caught her eye. They looked a little out of place, perhaps. But they were *really* good. Sparks seemed to fly when they rode together.

On Saturday, Marie sought out Harry between classes. Where had he gotten the funny horse with the unstoppable jumping style? she asked.

Harry was a little surprised to be approached by a newspaper writer. He was happy to share, in his heavily accented English, the story of the trip to New Holland just two years earlier, of finding the horse on the slaughterhouse truck. He specialized in buying cheap horses. Or green horses, rejects from here and there. He did not find anything extraordinary about it, he explained to Marie as she nodded and took notes.

But Marie saw something special. And she had a sense that, in Harry and Snowman, she might just have found the great news story she was looking for.

By Saturday afternoon, the gray horse and his brash young rider had attracted even more of a following.

Horses earned points for their wins in each class. Whichever horse had won the *most* points at the end of the three-day show would be declared the champion on Sunday, the show's final day. Now, on Day 2, Andante was slightly ahead. But Snowman was performing fantastically—enough to be considered a threat. If he won *this* class, he and Andante would be tied by the final jumper stakes.

A large crowd had gathered for the jumper class. Dave Kelley went first. He expertly guided his bay over the jumps. Andante looked every inch the seasoned competitor. When they pulled up at the end, the pair had only one fault.

Next up, Harry entered the ring, looking as calm as a man out for a country ride. The crowd stilled. To beat Andante, Snowman would need a clear round—a round with no faults. The gray had been jumping well all weekend, but this was his fourth class of the day—and the fences were formidable. On such a demanding course, after already putting out so much effort, an untested horse like Snowman might fall apart.

As Snowman circled the arena, there was no sound except the thump of his cantering hooves on the sand. There was a beat of silence as he passed over each fence, followed by the thump of landing. Approaching the last fence, the horse had no faults. Holding the spectators spellbound, the big gray galloped down toward the uneven wall of brush, then took off and soared. He had cleared the obstacle with daylight beneath him.

When his feet hit the ground on the far side of the fence, the crowd erupted in applause. But Harry did not hear. He was concentrating on the false step he'd felt as the horse landed. Snowman had overreached on the landing. He'd clipped the back of a front heel with a hind shoe, scraping hair and skin away. Harry looked down. Blood leaked from the horse's foreleg. At almost the same moment, Johanna jumped up from the stands and ran to the fence.

Harry hopped off and led the horse quickly back to the stable. Johanna and the children followed nervously behind. Back in the stall, Harry bent down to examine Snowy's wound. It was a deep gash across the pastern, too wide to stich closed. The pastern, the slender, sloped part of a horse's foreleg, takes much of the brunt when a horse lands. Any swelling there and the joint would stiffen up, making jumping impossible.

"What are you going to do?" Johanna finally said. "You won't be able to ride tomorrow."

But Harry was not licked yet. He had handled all kinds of equine emergencies. Gently, he probed the wound as the big gray lowered his head and snuffled. Harry knew that if he iced Snowy's leg, there was a chance, however small, that he could keep the swelling down. It was a long shot, however. And he'd have to work quickly.

Johanna took the children back home. Harry, meanwhile, climbed into his van and drove off to look for a gas station with an ice dispensary. He bought bags and bags of ice, hurrying back to Snowman before they could melt.

Back at the stable, Harry fashioned an ice pack. While the

other riders were out at show parties or back in their motels asleep, Harry squatted in the stall and kept watch. When he ran out of ice, he drove to the filling station for more. It was just him alone with his horse in the dark, straw-filled stall. Occasionally, he muttered a word or two to the horse in Dutch, but mostly the pair were quiet. No sound but the faint rustling as the horse shifted his weight or moved around in the straw.

Through the night, Harry cared for Snowman, catching only snatches of sleep. His muscles ached. When, in the early morning, the grooms arrived, he awoke, stiff from the night spent hunched in the corner against the rough wooden barn walls. He looked out at the sky. It was barely dawn. Time to see how the wound had fared overnight. Harry cut the ice pack away. Beneath his fingers he felt only the smooth sides of Snowman's lower foreleg—the pastern and the heel where the flesh met the rim of the hoof were firm and true, without a trace of swelling.

Harry watched closely for the telltale bobbing head of a hurt horse—but Snowman showed no hint of soreness. For the first time in what felt like hours, Harry allowed himself to exhale. He was overwhelmed with relief.

Still, there was no telling if Snowy would be able to take the stress of the high jumps in the stakes class. When a horse jumps, all of his thousand-odd pounds comes down on his two front legs. The higher the fence, the more pressure is applied to those slender forelegs. A horse who is injured or sore will be likely to falter on the landing. If a horse loses its balance, the risk of a gruesome fall—and a permanent injury—is much worse.

Harry spent the entire morning walking Snowman on a lead rope, then rubbing him down, then walking him more, trying to keep the gelding loose and limber so that the injured leg wouldn't stiffen up. Harry himself felt stiff in the saddle, like an old man. He had slept barely at all. Still, he took a deep breath and prepared for the competition ahead.

When it was time for the afternoon class, he carefully bandaged both of Snowman's front legs, then slipped rubber bell boots over Snowman's hooves to protect his heels. Finally, reassured that the horse was steady on his feet, Harry guided Snowman toward the schooling fence. The gelding gathered himself and soared—then landed and continued at a measured gallop. That's when Harry knew for *sure* that his horse was ready to compete.

Soon it was time for the final jumper stakes. By now, the crowd was paying attention, anticipating a showdown. Who would win? The reigning champion Andante, or the upstart Snowman? Even without being aware of Snowman's close brush with disaster, spectators had gotten behind the big gray horse. In the press box, Marie Lafrenz was one of many reporters present. Nobody wanted to miss a good story.

At the gate, Andante was keyed up. Her ears were pinned back, and she was nervously twitching her tail back and forth. But in spite of the mare's fidgeting, Dave Kelley looked completely cool. Holding the reins in one hand, his crop in the other, he sat loosely in the saddle. The relaxed grin of a winner spread across his face.

In the first go-through, both Andante and Snowman sailed to clear rounds, the only two horses to score no penalties.

Now it was time for the jump-off.

The crew moved quickly around the arena, raising the hurdles another six to eight inches. They also spread the jump supports farther apart, to create more width. After a few minutes, the jump-off course was ready. In spite of the horses' fatigue from three days of grueling competition, this was the most daunting course of the entire horse show.

Andante was up first. She catapulted into the ring with a burst, then bounded toward the first fence at a gallop. Kelley held the mare's nervous energy firmly in check. He kept the reins short and his calves wrapped tightly around her sides. At first, they seemed in unbeatable form, but when they got to the triple bar—a huge spread fence with bars stairstepping up in a steep incline—the pair failed to clear the top railing. It teetered for a moment, and then it fell.

Four faults.

This really *was* a difficult course. Even veteran Andante had been unable to go clean. The fences were all above five feet, with big spreads, and the horses were tired. And Snowman's sore leg was more likely to bother him now as the day was wearing on. To jump this raised course without any faults was going to be a challenge. If Snowman knocked down a pole, the horses would be tied. A tie would mean yet another round of jump-offs with even higher fences. It would also mean increasing the risk that one of the worn-out jumpers would take a misstep and crash.

When Harry rode into the ring on a loose rein, the contrast between the two horses' styles was impossible to miss. Captivated by the big gray with the easygoing manner, the crowd whooped its approval.

Harry headed toward the first fence at a controlled gallop. Snowman approached, nose outstretched. His ears pricked forward, with the same sweet expression he bore when running free in the paddock.

Over each fence, they went. Everyone in the crowd held their breath, exhaling only when the horse's hooves thumped on the landing. Harry flew into the air, but his weight stayed balanced over the horse. Together, they headed toward the high triple bar—and cleared it easily.

Down the line to the last fence, the big parallel bars, Harry galloped. He kept the reins loose. The big gray horse took off, soared . . . and flew over the last fence. Again, no faults! Harry, caught up in the excitement of the ride, suddenly understood what this meant: he and his lumbering plow horse had just won the championship stakes class. They had beaten Andante, the reigning champion!

The judges hunched over their scorecards, pencils scratching. A few moments later, the announcement came over the PA system: Snowman was the open jumper champion, winner of the stakes class and champion of the show! The great Andante had come in second. The trophy would be engraved with the names of a *new* team: Harry de Leyer and Snowman.

That evening, Harry pinned a tricolor ribbon next to Snowman's stall. Harriet, Marty, and Chef all gathered around the big gray. Snowy stretched his nose down to receive their pats and praise.

Marie Lafrenz had already captured the moment on her typewriter and sent off a press release. The next morning, her article ran in the *Herald Tribune* under the headline THE CINDERELLA HORSE. The story of the plow horse's triumph was repeated over and over again. Before he left the show that day, Dave Kelley came by to congratulate Harry. Dave was never a sore loser. As always, his congratulations were genuine. He loved a good contest and respected others for their victories.

"You should come up to Fairfield," he said to Harry with a big smile. "I think you and your plow horse can win it."

Harry smiled, but he felt a flutter of nervousness. Fairfield, in Connecticut, was another powerhouse of talent on the East Coast circuit. He'd have to talk it over with Johanna. It was one thing to go to some of the local shows—there were several good ones within a short distance of their home—but following the circuit required a much higher level of commitment.

The 1950s was not a time when people got caught up in foolishness and chased big dreams. It was a time of conformity. Big, expensive, whimsical aspirations were the province of the rich—people who had time, money, and fewer responsibilities.

But some people automatically lift their eyes above the horizons and see more. Harry was such a person. In the lift and thrust that powered Snowman over fences, Harry sensed the same belief in his horse: a conviction that you can soar if you want to; you just have to want it badly enough.

CHAPTER 15

NEW CHALLENGES

WESTPORT, CONNECTICUT, 1958

Joe Keswyzk and Jim Troutwell weren't exactly grooms. The two local men helped out around Harry's barn, and sometimes went with him to shows as well. Joe drove a big truck during the week and pitched in with the horses on weekends. Jim worked nights, then came over early in the morning to lend a hand. Jim was dark-haired, a sign of his Native American roots; Joe was blue-eyed and fair. Both men were over six feet tall and burly. Harry, with his medium stature and slim build, looked small next to the pair of friends. Joe and Jim had turned into Snowman's biggest fans, and they had a prediction: Snowman, they said, was going to take the championship at the Fairfield horse show.

After his Sands Point victory, Snowman had stirred up interest in the press. Local papers were all over the story of this gentle gray horse. Everyone was anticipating his appearance at the upcoming Fairfield show.

Back at Hollandia, Harry readied Snowman for Fairfield,

along with Night Arrest, and the pretty chestnut Wayward Wind. As the weather threatened rain, Harry loaded up the trio of horses. The two grooms climbed into the van with them, and off they went to Connecticut. The de Leyers wouldn't consider leaving the family behind, and so Johanna and the children would meet Harry at the show in Westport, Connecticut.

Harry had never left Long Island for a show before. Here, he would be facing a whole new set of rivals. There was Adolph Mogavero from Ox Ridge Hunt Club—one of the biggest and most competitive operations on the East Coast. Ox Ridge's young Thoroughbred mare, First Chance, had cleaned up at shows last spring. Andante, the tough old warrior, would also be there. They were all serious competition.

Harry had a very busy day ahead of him. He had entered Wayward Wind and Night Arrest in the green jumpers for first-timers. And with Night Arrest and Snowman, Harry would even be competing against himself in the open jumpers. That meant he'd ride the two horses almost back-to-back. Riding more than one horse in a class was tricky. Harry would have to rely on Jim and Joe's help. As he hopped off one horse, Harry would hand the reins to his grooms, then jump right on the other one. The horses had different skills. Night Arrest was a flashy and talented dark dapple gray whose thoroughbred breeding and high-strung temperament gave her terrific speed—an advantage whenever time was a factor. But she could be a handful, unlike the steady Snowy.

As usual, Snowman seemed nonchalant. It was always nice to have him along because he calmed the other horses. Harry knew that most people considered Snowman's victory at Sands Point a fluke. Sure, the odds were against him. But in the de

Leyer household, Snowman was the favorite. The whole family believed he could do it again.

The first open jumper class was held early on Friday morning, June 20, the show's opening day. This would be Snowman's first time up against the young mare First Chance. A lot of people were predicting that First Chance would be a strong contender for the national championship.

By the time the first class started, the rain was coming down hard. Luckily, the footing was still solid and not too slippery. After the first round, Andante had knocked down a pole. Out of the entire field, only Snowman and First Chance had had clean rounds.

There weren't many people on the grounds that morning. Rain had kept away most of the spectators, so there were just the riders, trainers, owners, and their families. Johanna and the children huddled together under an umbrella, watching intently.

Between the rounds, the grooms cleaned up Snowman, rubbing down his legs with a soft cloth. His gray coat glowed softly in the rain.

Meanwhile, the jump crew, their white uniforms already splashed and muddy, raised the bars.

When Harry came into the ring for the jump-off, nobody was paying attention except Johanna and the children. But Snowman, seemingly unperturbed by the rain, sailed around the course for another clean round. When First Chance came into the ring, she flew around the course, too. Back came the jump crew, scurrying around to raise the bars higher.

For the next round, the height was now a daunting five feet, six inches.

First Chance knocked down a pole. Snowman went clean.

Johanna and the children jumped up from their seats in delight. The plow horse had won another blue ribbon!

Maybe the victory at Sands Point hadn't been a fluke after all.

Next up were the green jumpers, a class for horses competing for the first time. Since Snowman had been to a show the previous fall, he wasn't eligible. This time, Harry would be riding Night Arrest and Wayward Wind, one after the next. The rain continued steadily, and helmetless Harry just kept riding. When the water dripped down his forehead, he wiped it away with the arm of his tweed jacket.

At the end of the green jumpers class, Harry had collected another two ribbons for Hollandia—a blue for Night Arrest and a second-place red for Wayward Wind.

With each ribbon, more and more horse fans were catching wind of Harry de Leyer.

The next day, a steady summer downpour kept hammering the show grounds. The rain had scared off all but the most dedicated spectators. Men wore tweed hats and full-length raincoats. Women carried black umbrellas and wore muckers to wade through the mud.

The day before, the footing on the polo field had been decent. Today it was soupy, the worst possible conditions for jumping. Big puddles were collecting on the surface of the sandy ring. The most dangerous situation for a jumping horse is unsure footing—sliding on takeoff would ensure a crash. Perhaps even worse. Sliding on landing could bring a horse to the ground, possibly crushing the rider's leg under his thousand-pound body. Often, the worst injuries to riders occurred when a horse fell, then hit the rider's unprotected head with his iron-shod hooves as he was scrambling to his feet. Helmets weren't standard in the 1950s.

But Harry wasn't too worried about the footing. He had years of experience riding with the Knox girls out in the hilly wooded fields around Smithtown with the hunt. Knowing that his mount was sure-footed and used to galloping in rain, even snow, over muddy bogs and sandy flats, made him trust his horse. Harry was confident that Snowman, more than any other competitor, would be comfortable galloping through soupy sand.

In all the excitement, the competitions seemed to fly by. The first class of the morning was the knock-down-and-out class. Any competitor who knocked down a pole would be eliminated. When it was Snowman's turn, the de Leyers clapped louder than anyone in the small crowd. Snowman went clean on the first round, to Harry's delight.

Next up, they found themselves back in a jump-off against First Chance. Snowman couldn't seem to hit his stride and ended up taking down a pole. Still, Harry was happy that they won the red ribbon. He patted the horse on the neck as he exited the ring. The grooms kept busy, scraping mud off the horses between each round.

By now, there were seven classes leading up to the championship. So far, Snowman had won a ribbon in all of them.

On Sunday, the last day of the show, the rain clouds finally broke up. Sun streamed down on the polo field. Most of the soupy puddles started to dry up. As the weather cleared, the fans who had stayed home on Friday and Saturday came out to see the show. A festive energy was spreading through the arena.

The big jumps were set up for the championship classes. Harry stood by the side of the ring, surveying the course.

Going into the stakes class, two horses were vying for the title: Snowman and First Chance.

Whichever horse won the class would bring home the show championship. First Chance—younger, lighter-boned, and pretty—was having a great season. Her rider, Adolph Mogavero, was a seasoned pro. Fairfield was almost home turf for them. Mogavero had shown here at Fairfield numerous times.

Snowman was heavier-boned than First Chance, and he had the unfortunate setback of not only age but less experience. This would be his second-ever stakes class. After three days of slogging through the rain, Harry was not sure how much energy the horse had left. But Snowman seemed to like performing in front of a crowd, and had an eager look in his eye.

Right from the start of the jumper stakes, it was clear that the crowd had a favorite: Harry and his bulky gray horse. Some fans had read about them in the paper, and others were simply charmed by the handsome young man with the bright eyes and big smile.

All the horses—First Chance and Andante, Bon Soir and the other Thoroughbreds—lined up at the in-gate. Joe and Jim had Night Arrest and Wayward Wind ready to go. The horses paced as the grooms walked them in circles, trying to keep them calm while they waited. The fences in the stakes class were formidable, all between five and a half and six feet tall.

Each time a horse sailed over a fence, everyone in the crowd gasped and held their breath.

Harry was first up on Wayward Wind. He brought home a clear round, then tossed the reins to the groom and jumped on Night Arrest. The crowd clapped, delighted to see Harry ride again. Night Arrest danced and pranced when she entered the ring, like a bundle of energy. Again, another clear round for Harry de Leyer. A few more horses went, and then it was Snowman's turn. The crowd had already seen Harry charge around the course twice, on the two Thoroughbreds. Snowman turned his head and appeared to survey the crowds—perhaps looking for Johanna and the children up in the bleachers, cheering him on.

Harry smiled in the direction of the stands, then eased the horse into an easy canter. There were still a few puddles on the ground, and the footing was sticky. Still, Snowman cantered confidently around the course, completely in sync with his rider. Over the last fence, a huge set of parallel bars, Snowman jumped up and sailed over with room to spare. Harry could hear a woman on the sidelines gasp.

Harry and Snowman's performance brought down the house. It was official: Snowman had won the championship—again! And he won reserve champion with Night Arrest in the open jumpers.

This weekend, ribbons and silver plates were piled on the front seat of the car. The win was a couple hundred dollars—enough to cover their expenses, with a bit to spare. The long drive up to Connecticut, the money for gas, and the grooms' pay—it had all been worth it.

After Fairfield, horse show fever hit the de Leyer household. School was out for the summer, Knox was closed, and the de Leyer family caravan became a familiar sight at every show.

Everything the de Leyers did, they did together, and people smiled when pretty Johanna walked through the showgrounds, shepherding her friendly children in front of her. No matter how hot and dusty it was, Chef, Marty, and William were neatly groomed, as well turned out as the horses. Even tomboy Harriet always wore a clean dress.

From one horse show to the next, it was the same routine. Late nights, washing in preparation for the show. Early mornings, Harry up before four; and the long trailer trip to the next show. Everywhere from Connecticut to Long Island to New Jersey.

A few days later, the preparations would start again. The weeks passed in a whirlwind. And every weekend, on the way home, the dashboard of the old station wagon was covered with silken ribbons.

CHAPTER 16

PIPING ROCK, PART I: THE COMPETITION

LOCUST VALLEY, LONG ISLAND, 1958

In September 1958, the Piping Rock Horse Show was in its fifty-third year.

The drive from the de Leyers' converted chicken farm in St. James to the grounds of the Piping Rock Club wasn't long. But what a world away it was. Set along Long Island's Gold Coast, the area made famous by jazz-era novelist F. Scott Fitzgerald in *The Great Gatsby*, the Piping Rock Club prided itself on its cliquey exclusivity. This was where the elite of New York society gathered.

The entrance to Piping Rock wasn't much to see. Just two stone pillars that marked a winding path into the piney woods. But let there be no mistake. The humble entrance was designed with only one goal in mind: to turn away outsiders. According to the rules of the club, one needed to be invited inside in order to see the grandeur.

The United States was a land of increasing diversity and opportunity, but at this swanky establishment, there was no sign that change was coming. Behind the Piping Rock gates, out of sight, was one of the most elegant clubs on the Eastern Seaboard. Designed in 1913, the club had a rambling but elegant clubhouse that overlooked a courtyard with a fountain. The golf links were among the finest in the nation. The horse show's jumping contests were held in a beautiful grass arena the *New York Times* had called "the finest exhibition field in the world for the purpose."

The money prizes at Piping Rock were generous, attracting the top horses to the yearly event. But Piping Rock was devoted to the concept of amateur sport. The mind-set—that professionals were lesser than amateurs—went unquestioned. *Amateur* was a code word for the privileged class. Like the climbers who claimed victory at the top of Mount Everest—while hardly mentioning the local Sherpas who climbed along with them and carried their gear—it was the owners and amateur riders who were considered important at Piping Rock. Pros may have been allowed inside the ring now, but *professional* was still just another name for the hired help.

In short: the people of Piping Rock were not a welcoming bunch.

One of the most intimidating horseowners at Piping Rock was a woman named Eleo Sears. On the first morning at the Piping Rock Horse Show, she posed for a photo with her usual forthright gaze. She stood in the center, looking directly into the camera. Her face was shaded by her trademark white felt hat; her skin sported a perpetual suntan. She wore sensible heels, a skirt, a cardigan, and a white blouse. On each side of her stood a handsome young man wearing pegged breeches and riding boots, his velvet cap tucked under his arm. They were Bill Steinkraus and Frank Chapot, both members of the United States Equestrian Team. They had shown Miss Sears's horses successfully in Europe.

In the summer of 1958, Eleonora Randolph Sears had recently celebrated her seventieth birthday, yet still maintained the erect posture of an athlete. In fact, Eleo Sears had been one of the best-known female athletes of the early twentieth century. In addition to being a fearsome tennis champion, she was also famed at squash, had pioneered women's entry into polo, drove her own car in an era when few women did, and had even piloted a plane.

Prior to Miss Sears's time, women competed only in ladies' classes, riding and even jumping sidesaddle, an absurd feat that, while considered "more ladylike," was also much more difficult than jumping with both feet planted firmly in the stirrups. By 1958, Miss Sears was one of the most intimidating and powerful women in the horse world.

This time she no longer rode in the show but continued as a horse owner, and a spectator. Her two horses, Diamant and Ksar d'Esprit (pronounced kiss-AR dess-PREE), would be piloted by the two gentlemen stars flanking her in the photograph.

The press had been abuzz about the United States Equestrian Team's performances in Europe over the summer. The young American team had won the King George V Gold Cup in London—perhaps the most prestigious jumping competition in the world—taking home the team gold. It was a huge triumph. Ksar d'Esprit, with Bill Steinkraus aboard, and Diamant, ridden by Frank Chapot, had been among the top four competitors.

Steinkraus, a tall, slender man from Connecticut, was widely admired for his effortless elegance on horseback. And Frank Chapot, an Ivy Leaguer, was considered a fearless rider. For both of these horse-and-rider teams, showing at Piping Rock marked their official return to the United States. It was also the first stage of gearing up for the U.S. indoor season in the autumn, when the competition heated up even more at the National Horse Show.

Harry believed he could compete with the top competitors in show jumping, but according to the rules, because he earned a living teaching horseback riding, he was officially barred from joining the United States Equestrian Team, to compete in international competitions or to ride under the American flag in the Olympic Games. He might be as good or even better than Frank Chapot and William Steinkraus, but when it came to joining their team—he was not welcome.

Piping Rock introduced Harry to a whole other level of horse showing. Not just the cream of the crop from Europe but the best of Connecticut and Pennsylvania were there. Sure, it had been exciting to win back-to-back championships at North Shore and Sands Point, Lakeville and Fairfield. But now people in the crowd were talking about the equestrian team and its riders' performances in Europe. In comparison, the summer circuit seemed like small potatoes.

On the morning of September 10, 1958, Harry, Johanna, the children, and Snowman headed off to the Piping Rock Club certain of one thing: they would give it their best shot.

For Harry, the summer's end was bittersweet. While the rest

of the horses and riders would stay on the road all fall, Harry would have to return to his daily routine of tending to the barn and teaching lessons in the afternoon. His weekends would be taken up with small local shows with his pupils. Maybe he could get to a few of the bigger shows, but more or less, his show year was over.

Between now and then, however, there was Piping Rock. Snowman was sharp after the summer's competition and Harry knew not to overtrain him. A horse had only so many good jumps in him, after all. Harry did not want to take advantage of Snowy's good nature or ruin his legs. Harry wanted Piping Rock, the season's swan song, to be the horse's best show.

Every horse in the competition would be competing for ribbons. But only the top few would be in the running for the William S. Blitz Memorial Gold Challenge, a huge gold trophy awarded to the horse that won the most points during the entire three-day competition.

Over the years, the Blitz trophy seemed to practically belong to Eleo Sears. Her horses had won it in 1955 *and* 1956. The Blitz carried a one-thousand-dollar prize, a much bigger prize than most other cups. But the money prize would not have been of interest to Eleo, a great-granddaughter of Thomas Jefferson, whose family had been rich for generations. To Eleo Sears, one thousand dollars was nothing. In any case, she didn't even believe in prize money. She thought that people should compete for the love of the sport alone.

That was easy for *her* to say. Nobody who knew Harry de Leyer would contest that he loved the sport. But for the hard-working young father, that one-thousand-dollar prize would be an enormously helpful amount of money.

With Johanna's frugal accounting, the money would be put to good use. It was clear that the de Leyers needed to find a new home. The horses were splitting the chicken coop farm at the seams. One and a half acres was not enough room for all of them. Harry had his eye on a property that was larger—about five acres. By scrimping and saving every penny, they might be able to move to the bigger place.

For now, the de Leyers focused on the task at hand. Over the summer, competing week after week, the de Leyer family had learned to work like a well-oiled machine. They had their routine down pat. Johanna always had the family dressed to the nines, but when they arrived at the showgrounds, everyone changed into wooden shoes and coveralls. Even the children had a job to do. Harry got the stable set up, stacking bales and filling the stalls with fresh straw. The boys and Harriet carried buckets and brushes. With the help of Joe Keswyzk and Jim Troutwell, Hollandia's stabling area was spick-and-span. Snowman's impressive array of ribbons, tacked up next to his stall, livened up their stable area, too.

The big green horse van that Snowman traveled in was comfortable enough, but it could not begin to compare with the specially equipped airplane on which Eleo's horses had traveled home from Europe just a few days before. These were among the most pampered horses in the world.

Eleo Sears's horse Ksar d'Esprit, like Snowman, was a gray, but that was the only similarity between the two geldings. Ksar was slim and fine-boned, with a snappy action over fences and a lovely, refined Thoroughbred face. This horse was already a veteran of several European tours *and* a former champion at the National Horse Show. And Bill Steinkraus was an elegant and tactful rider as well as a Wall Street businessman and a concert violinist.

Steinkraus and Ksar d'Esprit on a good day were unbeatable. Harry had to hope that they would not be having a good day.

If possible, Miss Sears's other horse, Diamant, was even more impressive. Diamant was a German-bred jumper purchased from one of Germany's leading riders. The horse had already been a seasoned champion in Europe. He arrived at Piping Rock as a strong favorite. In any case, people figured that the main competition would be between the two young Olympians, mounted on two of the best horses in America.

Everyone else who entered did so at their own risk.

Snowman had been an entertaining diversion to audiences during the summer months, but now the fall equestrian season was in full swing. People who took the sport *really* seriously were there. Sure, the gray horse had won some championships, but against whom? Not these big shots. He'd had his moment in the sun, and the fans' interest returned to the glamorous boys of the United States Equestrian Team.

Harry de Leyer wasn't easily cowed by pretensions, though. He didn't concern himself with these things. When it came to riding, no amount of fancy qualifications could take the place of seat-of-the-pants skill. And to Harry, it wasn't his appearance or the opinions of others that mattered. The only thing that mattered was his belief in himself.

Harry had brought three horses to this show: Night Arrest and Wayward Wind to compete in the green jumpers, and Snowman to compete for the Blitz. The gray settled right into his stall, his calming presence helping keep the other two on an even keel. With his head hanging over the half door, he took in the scene with a gentle knowingness.

Snowman was braided up and spotlessly clean, groomed until his shiny late-summer coat showed dapples if the light reflected across it the right way. His whiskers had been trimmed and his hooves painted. Like the kids, he looked dressed up in his Sunday finery.

The children were excited as Harry bedded down his horse for the night. School would be starting soon, and their long summer spent following Snowman from show to show would come to an end. Harry loved their simple, dedicated belief in their pet. Only he and Johanna understood that their lesson horse had just stepped into a whole new level of competition.

This show would not pay for itself unless Snowman won the Blitz prize—and that meant he would have to be all-around champion across three days of grueling competition. As always, Snowman looked at his owner with the big brown eyes that had earned him the nickname Teddy Bear. Sometimes Harry felt that the old horse all but opened his mouth and talked to him. The gelding's steady dark gaze told Harry that he would do his best. Harry could not ask for more than that.

CHAPTER 17

PIPING ROCK, PART II: THE SHOW BEGINS

Friday dawned gray and cool, perfect riding weather. The bright green turf field was neatly groomed. Schooling jumps were set up out in the woods. Society folks lined up to watch the games begin.

All of the fences at Piping Rock were white: white standards, white poles. The jump crew dressed in white from top to toe. Harry kept busy around the stables, cleaning his gear. There was always work to be done. Even though Snowman was spotless, Harry went through the entire ritual: he picked the horse's feet, pinching the tendon gently and cleaning out the underside of the hoof. Next came the soft body brush, which drew up the skin's oils to bring out the coat's natural shine.

Even now, Harry could not work over this horse without remembering what he had looked like just a couple of years earlier. Judging him by his appearance, one would not think he was the same horse. But Harry knew the new look did not change him. Every horse was a combination of what you could see on the outside and what he carried with him on the inside.

Harry was like a proud father. Johanna always made sure that the children looked neat; Harry wanted Snowman to look his best, too.

Harry slipped a finger into the horse's mouth and slid the soft rubber snaffle into place, then folded down each ear in succession, settling the bridle's crownpiece into a comfortable position. The carefully oiled leather felt buttery and familiar under his callused fingers. He fastened the throat latch and gave his horse a pat on the neck. Harry's own riding breeches were spotless. He straightened his tie, slipped on his jacket, and slicked back his hair to ready it for his black velvet cap. One of the grooms came over with a cloth to shine the last of the dust off Harry's boots.

Maybe at ringside they looked like a couple of country bumpkins. Some looked down their noses at the pair. The rider lacked the perfectly tailored clothes and the upper-class ease of most of the other riders. The gelding was so clearly a grade horse. But in the ring, magic happened: the horse seemed almost to turn into a different animal, and the rider was magnetic to watch. They held the crowds spellbound.

There were two main series of classes during the Piping Rock Horse Show: the fault-and-out classes and the Blitz Memorial Series.

In fault-and-out classes, horses would be judged on speed. Touching the fence would not count—only a horse that knocked down a pole or refused a fence would get a penalty. The fences were high and a rider was rewarded for keeping the horse tightly leashed and making turns in the air and short approaches to fences.

The bigger challenge was the second group of classes: the Blitz Memorial Series. In these, even the lightest brush of hoof to railing would be penalized.

Miss Sears's Ksar d'Esprit would compete in the fault-and-out series, while her big German horse, Diamant, would go for the Blitz trophy. Harry had entered Snowman in *both* series. The big gray would not have the opportunity to rest as much between classes. But Harry had no choice. The only way to cover the cost of the horse show was to win prize money. The more classes they competed in, the higher chance they had of winning. And Harry knew Snowman was a strong horse, his muscles honed by pulling a plow.

For the competition's first jumper class, the stands were still almost empty. But Harry spotted Marie Lafrenz in the crowd, tapping away at her typewriter. Eleo Sears was also easy to pick out. Perched in the bleachers near the front, she kept her ice-blue eyes on the ring.

The fault-and-out series was run on the rules normally used in international shows, where performance was judged both on ability to clear the fences and on the horse's time. These international rules favored a different kind of horse—one that could accelerate quickly, turn sharply, and gain enough momentum to clear both height and width—with only a short distance to prepare. Harry knew he would have to cut corners to get a fast-enough time to win.

The course was intimidating: the all-white fences glared in the sun, and the turf footing was sometimes slippery. The

last jump was a big rounded obstacle just twenty-four feet beyond the previous fence. That combination would be a tight
in-and-out. And it'd be especially difficult since horses would
be headed toward the out-gate, in the direction of the stables,
making them more prone to want to speed ahead.

Bill Steinkraus entered the ring on Ksar d'Esprit. He sailed
around the course with no faults, looking every bit the veteran
Olympian he was.

When Harry entered the ring on Snowman, he knew he
had reason to worry. With his relaxed manner and long, lanky
stride, Snowman wasn't a natural for classes based on speed.
Snowman liked to jump clean, but he had not been bred for
racing and was not as naturally fast as some of the other horses.
To beat Ksar d'Esprit, Snowman would have to clear all the
hurdles with no jumping faults—and he'd have to do it in less
time than it had taken Ksar d'Esprit to complete the course.

Harry guided the horse through the tight turns, and Snowman followed Harry's lead, but he just wasn't sharp. Over the
second-to-last fence, he dropped a hind leg, knocking a pole
from its cup.

Exiting the ring, Harry saw his children's disappointed
faces. After so many wins in a row, it was hard to watch the big
gray get crushed by Ksar d'Esprit, a horse who was so much
better known and finely bred. But Harry lost no time thinking
about his defeat. He needed to get Snowman cooled down and
comfortable. The Blitz Memorial Series started in the afternoon. They would be competing against Miss Sears's other formidable entry, Diamant.

*   *   *

The rest of the morning flew by, and before long, it was time to start the routine again: grooming, saddling, and bridling. When Snowman was ready, Harry headed out to the schooling area and nodded hello at his competitors. The glossy brown Diamant thundered across the schooling ring impressively— he was a big horse and you could see his fine breeding in his powerful haunches and heavy bones. When the veteran gelding entered the ring with Frank Chapot on board, there was no sign of skittishness. With the precision of a German clock, the pair turned in an effortless, perfect round.

Snowman was up. Reins loose, Harry crouched low over the horse. He urged Snowy into a gallop toward the big white triple bar. This was going to be a tricky jump. Each pole was a stairstep above the one in front of it. The poles seemed to float in the air, making it hard for both horse and rider to judge their distance as they approached.

Since the fence was wide as well as tall, arriving at just the right spot for takeoff was very important. Several horses had already misjudged. They'd taken off a stride early and knocked down the back pole. Others had realized their misjudgment and galloped an extra stride. But then their horses couldn't snap their knees up quickly enough, and they'd plowed right through the first pole.

As Snowman sailed over the big jump, his knees were tucked up so that he had at least a foot to spare. Harry's face disappeared into the horse's outstretched neck. At the end of the first round, two horses had gone clean: the massive German import and the gray plow horse.

The jump crew raised the fences for the next round.

Diamant was to jump first, and the crowd quieted as he

entered the ring. He was all business as he pounded down to the first fence. At the sidelines, Miss Sears leaned forward slightly. It was all over in a minute. Diamant was clear, with what appeared to be little effort on his part. This horse was unstoppable.

As Harry and Snowman trotted into the ring, the contrast was inescapable. Harry grinned at the children perched on the fence, then smiled at the crowd; his horse, seeming to sense that this was a performance, turned his gaze there, too. The spectators responded with a smattering of enthusiastic applause, then fell silent. This was a challenging course. Would this clunky horse really be up to the task?

Harry held Snowman's reins loosely. Careful observers noticed that he whispered something to his mount and that periodically one of the horse's ears would flick back: the horse was listening. As the horse bore down on the first fence, more than five and a half feet straight up, the crowd was attentive.

The horse lengthened his neck—one stride, two, three— then drew his haunches underneath him. Harry seemed almost to disappear over the fence, his lithe frame so lightly balanced that it was hard to tell where man ended and horse began. In a flash, the gray landed with a thump. Harry's eyes brought the line of the next fence into sight and then raised up above it. Like all good riders, he looked off in the distance beyond the fence, not at the ground.

After he had sailed over the last fence, there was a hush, as though nobody could quite believe their eyes. Then came the sharp rat-a-tat of applause. Again, Snowman was clean.

Miss Sears's ice-blue eyes watched intently from under her white hat. A sportsman to the core, she always enjoyed a good challenge. No one could deny that this little nobody of a horse was allowing her prize horse to show off his skill, the little gray David facing off against the mighty German Goliath.

It was time for the next jump-off. The white-clad fence crew raised the fences once more. The bigger horse, who stood over seventeen hands tall, now had a clear advantage. Each time a horse jumped a single fence, he was hefting twelve hundred pounds into the air. It was a one-on-one showdown, and now even the lowest fence was over five and a half feet.

This class had become a grueling test of stamina. Electric excitement coursed through the air. People gathered as word circulated among the spectators. *That eighty-dollar horse is still in the running!* they murmured.

Chapot and Diamant had both performed in front of Olympic crowds. Both had represented their countries, galloping under their country's flags. Anyone with a passing knowledge of horseflesh would bet on the Olympian. But a feeling of excitement was growing around the underdog horse and his smiling rider.

The crowd watched with growing pleasure as Snowman sailed around the course, making it look easy. Over the last hurdle, Harry let go of the reins entirely—a spectacular sight over a nearly six-foot fence. Snowman had made a third clean round. Now it was up to Diamant to match the gray's performance.

And match it he did. Galloping like a contained ball of fury, he rounded the course with style. The crowd fell silent. As his hooves thundered down, leaving another clean jump behind him, the crowd took a collective gasp. As Chapot bore down on the last fence, he looked as if he was almost home free—but not quite. On the big triple bar, Diamant got sloppy and just nicked the pole with his hind leg. The white pole teetered. Then, as if in slow motion, it fell.

The crowd paused in silence for a moment before erupting.

No one could believe it. The eighty-dollar wonder horse had just beaten the champion!

As Snowman paraded into the ring, the crowd went wild, clapping and cheering in a manner more fit for a baseball game than the manicured lawns of Piping Rock. Up in the press box, Marie Lafrenz tapped away on her typewriter, a small smile playing on her lips.

She'd gotten her story.

A parade of reporters with notebooks and pencils came around to talk to Harry, too. The next day, the sports pages were buzzing about him and his horse. Sports fans love to root for an underdog—in Snowman, they had found an under-horse. And Harry the riding teacher had acquired a new nick-name, too: the Flying Dutchman. Word was getting around about the plow horse who had beaten Eleo Sears's best Olym-pic prospect.

Harry was happy to answer questions as long as they didn't interfere with his work. He wanted to stay focused. After all, he hadn't won the show *yet*. To win the Blitz Memorial trophy, he'd have to have the highest score over the course of the full three days.

On Saturday, the show's second day, the weather was hot and the sky was bright blue. Spectators flocked to the club grounds. Members sat in boxes. Even ordinary folk were allowed onto the grounds to watch if they bought a ticket. They had all gathered for the main event: the first day of the Blitz Memorial Gold Challenge.

Not wanting to tire his horse, Harry barely had Snowy jump at all, just took a few turns around the ring to loosen the gray's legs. He noticed Chapot schooling Diamant, and the determined expression on the sportsman's face. Once again, the German horse looked unstoppable in the schooling ring. But Diamant and Snowman were not the only two horses in the class. The seven-year-old mare First Chance—ridden by Adolph Mogavero, Harry's chief competitor at Fairfield—could also hold her own in any competition.

Today's course looked even more intimidating than yesterday's. There were more fences. Higher ones, too. The series of obstacles played like a movie in Harry's head. He could already feel the rhythm of his horse's gallop.

Already, several horses had been eliminated at a big brush-wall-gate fence. Harry knew that this fence—which would have both height and width to jump over—would be his toughest challenge.

When Diamant came into the ring, Harry rode over to watch. The horse was jumping well, but when he reached the brush-wall-gate, he tapped the rail with a front foot, giving him one fault. Harry stroked Snowman's neck. The only way to beat Diamant without a jump-off would be to clear the first round with no faults.

That meant there was no room for error.

Despite the pressure, Harry entered the ring on a loose rein. Past the grandstand, Snowman pricked up his ears and glanced at the spectators, then turned to catch sight of the de Leyer children.

Harry cued Snowman to gallop, and they took off. As they approached the brush-wall-gate fence, Harry saw the problem. From the horse's perspective, the fence was a hanging gate with a brush box behind it. The white pole hidden behind the brush box *actually* turned the fence into a spread (meaning a fence that was both tall and wide). But the horse would not perceive that. So far, Snowman had always excelled at high and narrow fences. He had a short arc and tucked his knees up tight. He was a master at vertical height, but wide-spread fences caught him by surprise. This fence was going to be tricky.

Steady, steady, Harry thought, his hands sensing the power of the horse underneath him, gathering up, getting ready. Harry waited for the horse, trusted in him.

"You can do it, boy," he whispered.

Snowman collected his stride and sank back on his haunches, ready to clear the tippy-top of the brush. But even on takeoff, Harry could tell something was not right. The horse had not seen the hidden white pole. His arc was too tight. He rapped the heavy wooden pole with both legs. Hard. As the pole flipped to the side, Snowman faltered on the landing and took a jagged step. Four faults.

The crowd sat in stunned silence.

Harry exhaled. He reached over and patted his horse on the neck. "It's okay, boy," he whispered. In a split-second calculation, Harry realized they were already out of the ribbons. It would be better to pull up, he decided. Let the horse go back to his stall and rest, rather than finish out the course just to soothe Harry's own pride.

Harry saluted to the judge and then, patting his horse on the neck, trotted toward the out-gate. The gate man swung the gate open and the pair left the ring. Snowman was eliminated. Diamant would hold his lead to win the class.

The children were crushed, but Harry took the opportunity to make the loss into a lesson. Their horse was up against the toughest competition in America—perhaps in the world. He had jumped bravely yesterday, going to a third-round jump-off. And even though speed was not his natural style, he had won an FEI (Fédération Equestre Internationale) time class.

Diamant was ahead on points now. He had a first and a second, and Harry had only a first. The only way for Snowman to take home the Blitz prize would be to win the championship class, though the fences would be even higher, the pressure even more intense.

The mood in the barn that evening was quiet, but Harry went about his chores with his usual care.

Predictably, Diamant's name was emblazoned across the sports page headlines in the morning. The excitement around Snowman, the underdog, was forgotten. No one expected a comeback.

But, Harry thought, *tomorrow is another day*.

CHAPTER 18

PIPING ROCK, PART III: UP AND OVER

The final class of the Blitz Memorial Gold Challenge was held the next day, on Sunday afternoon. This would be the toughest course of all.

It had been a great summer, a season of glorious triumphs. Today was the very last day before the Knox school year started again.

This next class, the most important class of the season, carried a prize big enough to help Harry and Johanna buy a new farm. All the de Leyers knew what a big deal this could be for the family. Marty threw his arms around one of the horse's big legs while Harriet and Chef each whispered good-luck wishes. Harry looked deeply into the horse's dark eyes. This horse had his own wisdom. Even though Harry had seen the hurt in his children's eyes, he still thought he had made the right decision to pull up yesterday. Take care of your horse and he'll take care of you. Harry firmly believed that.

It was a hot day, the last gasp of summer, and Harry was uncomfortably warm under his hunt coat. He took a deep breath and swung up into the saddle, taking care to settle lightly on Snowy's back. Jim Troutwell ran a rag over Harry's boots and offered up a smile.

"Don't let the bigger horse get the better of you," he said.

Harry nodded appreciatively. Then he walked toward the schooling area. Chapot and Diamant were already there, under Miss Sears's watchful eye.

Snowman was rested and fresh, and he'd always risen to the challenge before. Harry was ready.

The stands were full as the Piping Rock Show drew to its close. The table that held the silver trophies was now empty but for the big gold Blitz cup winking in the September sun. It was such a challenging course that even some of the best horses—First Chance and Andante—were getting faults. Harry watched the other performances, seeing where the pitfalls lay. Thankfully, that brush-wall-gate obstacle wasn't there again. Still, the floating triple bar, the dome-shaped fence, and the parallel bars all presented major challenges of their own.

In this class, Snowman would go before Diamant. He would have to perform at his very best—without knowing how the other horse would do.

Harry heard the announcer call his name over the PA. He was on deck, up next. Snowman stood still on a loose rein, his ears lopped to each side in his trademark relaxed pose. Harry surveyed the crowds, catching sight of Eleo Sears standing near the fence, and Johanna and his children lined up in the bleachers.

"Snowman, owned by Mr. and Mrs. Harry de Leyer, ridden

by Harry de Leyer," said the announcer, summoning the pair into the ring. Harry slid his hands up the laced reins and squeezed his calves gently around the horse's barrel.

"This is it, Teddy Bear," he whispered to the horse, and one gray ear flicked back, attuned to his master's voice. Harry knew how crucial it was to keep a horse together on the last fence of the last class of the last day of the show—but especially in a big-money class that promised a huge gold cup as the prize.

Snowman walked into the ring, and Harry gave him a chance to look up at the crowd. *Let's make it a good one*, he thought, and then all thought disappeared. At a controlled gallop, Harry headed toward the first fence. He all but vanished into the flow—hoofbeats, fast, shifting turns where the horse made flying lead changes. *Up and over*, thump, thump, *up and over*. With each fence, the crowd seemed to hold its collective breath.

It was over in a moment. Only then did Harry realize they had done it. Snowman had gone clean. Now *he* was the horse to beat. Maybe living through a war makes a man philosophical, but Harry figured that he and his horse had done all they could do. He could control how well he rode and how well he cared for his horse, but he could not control what others did.

Harry saw the big brown horse Diamant head into the main ring. As the horse approached the first jump, Harry stopped to watch. It was hard to believe *anyone* could beat this horse. He was as tightly coiled and precise as a machine. The American horses looked practically like ponies by comparison.

As Chapot carefully rounded the course, the horse leapt over each fence with the same methodical jumping style. Finally, they headed toward the last fence. The horse bore down just a little faster than before, just a shade. He sank down on his hocks, then sprang up, his hindquarters shooting off like well-oiled pistons. But before it actually happened, before the crowd knew, before the press finished mentally composing the DIAMANT TRIUMPHS headline, Diamant flattened his arc just a bit too much. One hind foot lightly brushed the back pole. The pole teetered in place but held.

One half fault, for a hind touch.

That meant Snowman had done it. He had beat Diamant!

A few minutes later, Harry stood on the grass in the center of the ring. With one hand, he held Snowman's bridle. With the other, he patted the horse on the neck. He paused to smile at Johanna and wave to the children, but then he turned his mind back to Snowman. He could almost hear the murmur in the crowd: *Who is that? Is that the one they call the Flying Dutchman? Have you ever heard of him? I heard he bought that horse for only eighty dollars.*

Snowman blinked sleepily as the cameras flashed around him. Harry cradled the big gold cup in his arms, then raised it up for his horse to take a look. While they pinned a rosette to his bridle, Snowman stood quietly, as if wondering what all the fuss was about.

Over at the stables, Harry was already back in his coveralls. He and Jim Troutwell packed up, hefting gear and hay bales into the van. Snowman had his shipping bandages and blanket on. He was ready for a ride home and a well-earned rest. But on the front seat of the station wagon sat a tricolor ribbon. And in the clubhouse of the Piping Rock Club, the big gold Blitz Memorial trophy would soon be engraved with the name of a newcomer, a Dutch immigrant named Harry de Leyer, and his slaughterhouse-refugee horse, Snowman.

CHAPTER 19

THE INDOOR CIRCUIT

ST. JAMES, LONG ISLAND, FALL 1958

Back at the de Leyer house, Johanna had started a scrapbook with clippings of Snowman's adventures. Trophies and ribbons decorated the living room. But now it was back to routine at the Knox School. Even though the giddy summer had passed in a flash and the big gray horse had returned a champion, there was no sign that Harry's fellow teachers at Knox were impressed. Education was a serious business to them. Whatever horse show frippery he may have indulged in over vacation was of little interest to them. If they had seen the pictures or read the headlines, they gave no sign.

Snowman returned to his stall in the semicircular stable. He seemed perfectly content to carry the girls in their lessons. The days continued balmy and sunny through the first few weeks of September, and Harry enjoyed his teaching schedule even though the girls also gave no notice of Snowman's summer triumphs.

Harry put Snowman right back into the lesson lineup at Knox. His old schedule wasn't hard to readjust to. At night, at home with Johanna, though, Harry plotted out his double life of teaching at Knox and showing horses. There were a few more local weekend horse shows he could go to that autumn— but the rest of the season looked hopeless.

Right now, Snowman was in the lead to win the year's biggest trophy, the Professional Horsemen's Association (PHA) Championship, awarded to the highest-scoring horse and rider of the year. But Harry knew that he and Snowman would quickly lose their lead. The horses fighting for the PHA trophy would spend the fall chasing points at the biggest shows of the year, first in Harrisburg at the Pennsylvania National, then down to Washington, DC, for the Washington International, and last of all, the most important competition of the year—the National Horse Show held at Madison Square Garden in New York City. Horses would be racking up points faster than ever at these shows. At one competition alone, a horse that did well could match the points earned over the entire summer season. With Harry's responsibilities at work, there was no way that he and Snowman could maintain their lead.

Harry looked bleakly at the calendar: a day to drive to Harrisburg, another day to drive back, and seven days of show. The same thing for Washington. It was just too much time to take off from work at Knox. His boss would never allow it.

He needed his job at Knox for money. That was simply a fact. Even if Harry and Snowman won every class they entered, he could not earn enough prize money to support the horses and his family. And truthfully, he was grateful to have the job, grateful that the swank school had taken a chance on someone like him—an immigrant who was just learning English, and who had no social connections.

So, Harry put away the glorious quest of summer. He tried not to think about the other horses and riders who would still be competing for the prize. There was no point in feeling sorry for himself, so he worked to put the competitions out of his mind. Sure, in the mornings, up early, working alongside Jim Troutwell, cleaning stalls, he thought about the PHA Championship. When was the last time a horse in the lead for the trophy had dropped out of the competition? Probably never. Luckily, Harry couldn't dwell on that question. He was busy with his work, his family, and the hard effort of caring for his horses. He had no time to think about the horse shows that he and Snowman were going to miss.

Maybe somebody else in Harry's position would have felt thwarted. Here he was, on the cusp of an unthinkable triumph, and he had to fold his hand. And while Harry loved riding, competing, and winning trophies, he loved his job as a riding instructor, too. He stood in the sun in the middle of the arena on hot days. He stood in the courtyard getting wet when it rained. Day in, day out, Harry was there with his students, watching them, analyzing their riding styles, and sharing his wisdom. And Snowman was a teacher, too. Any girl who needed him climbed aboard the big gray teddy bear and grew more self-assured and braver in her riding. Compared to where they had been, both Harry and Snowman had a good life.

Yet, each day, when Harry headed out to the stable, he thought about the summer's triumphs, and of Snowman's performance against the toast of Europe. It felt wrong. The horse had been put on a shelf before he'd had a chance to show the world what he could do. Sure, he was a hundred times better off now than he'd been as a plow horse. But this horse could *jump*. At Knox, he was using only a small part of his talent carrying the lesson girls around the stable. Harry couldn't stop daydreaming about when they'd won the gold Blitz trophy, and what it felt like to parade Snowman around that swank arena at Piping Rock.

By the end of September, Harry had resolved to do something.

Dave Kelley was beloved on the horse show circuit: a true sportsman, a talented rider, and a straight shooter—a man to be trusted. He and Harry had become friends, running into each other at horse shows around the East Coast. So, Harry proposed a plan to him.

Snowman deserved a chance to see what he could do. And since Harry had to stay home and tend to his duties, what if *Dave* took Snowman on the road? The Washington International Horse Show—the last big contest before the Garden—was coming up. And a rider like Dave paired with a horse like Snowman might just be a winning combination.

October 10–15, 1958, was just another ordinary week at the Knox School, but the barn seemed empty with Snowman gone. Dave Kelley had loaded the horse into the van and taken him to Washington, DC. He'd happily agreed to Harry's plan. Now the de Leyers would have to follow the show's progress the same way everyone else did: in the newspapers.

Dave agreed to enter Snowman into the open jumper division. The lineup was impressive, with excellent teams from both

Mexico and Germany competing. But people hoping to see the Americans triumph were quickly disappointed. The U.S. team members performed poorly—complete with knocked-down fences, crashes, and falls. By the last night of the show, the team had managed to collect only two ribbons—a third and a fourth.

Then, during the evening performance, Frank Chapot, riding one of Eleo Sears's horses, crashed spectacularly on the final fence—a fall so devastating that the crowd paused in horror, unsure whether anyone would walk away. Fortunately, neither horse nor rider was seriously hurt.

In the open jumper classes, Snowman had a new rival. A high-strung half Thoroughbred named Windsor Castle, he looked more talented than Snowman—by a lot. The two horses battled it out. Snowman won the first class but lost to Windsor Castle in the second, putting Windsor Castle into the lead for the show championship.

Dave called Harry to give him the news. Snowman needed to win the next class—the stakes class—or he'd no longer be in the lead for the Horse of the Year award.

Back in St. James, Harry waited for Dave's nightly telephone call, with his reports of Snowman's performance. Harry was grateful to Dave, and yet he could not help feeling that maybe if *he* were there . . . the horse's familiar rider . . . but there was no use thinking about that. He had responsibilities that came before winning blue ribbons. Windsor Castle was tough competition, and Dave was not making any promises.

On October 15, the show's last night, the giant gates of the armory show ring swung open. Again, an impressive crowd of dignitaries and fans had gathered. Even President Dwight D. Eisenhower sat in the presidential box.

First into the ring was the German team, carrying the German flag. The four horsemen, who together had taken every single championship ribbon in the international competition, stopped under the glowing spotlights and saluted. Next up was the talented Mexican team. They, too, had collected more ribbons than the Americans.

That night in front of the president, Frank Chapot, perhaps still sore from his horrible crash of the night before, rode Trail Guide, one of the greatest horses ever to compete for the United States Equestrian Team. Trail Guide triumphed in the jump-off against Germany—the only win of the show for the American team.

Last up on the agenda was the crowd-pleasing favorite: the open jumper championship. Snowman needed to win this class or he would lose his lead for the championship.

When Snowman, the underdog favorite, entered the ring, the crowd let out a cheer. Snowman represented every little guy: everyone not sitting in a VIP seat, every worker at the armory that night—pushing a wheelbarrow or a broom—and everybody who was not born into privilege who competed in the ring that night. Dave knew this horse needed to win. He wanted to have good news when he called de Leyer at home. The pressure was intense.

As the crowd cheered, Dave Kelley rode the big gray gelding across the arena until he reached the foot of the presidential box. Doffing his velvet hunt cap, he saluted the president. Then, gathering his reins up tight, he urged Snowman into a canter.

There was so much to distract a horse here in the armory— the Army Marching Band; the thousands of spectators; the spotlights; the ring steward, sounding his long brass horn. But

Dave had a job to do, and Snowman seemed to sense it. As the gelding soared over each fence under the gleaming spotlights, he captivated the crowd. Like Trail Guide, Snowman's dignity had nothing to do with class or breeding, and everything to do with heart. None of the other horses—not Windsor Castle, not First Chance—could match the gray horse's performance that night. In the last class of the night, with the president of the United States of America in attendance, Snowman brought home the championship.

Snowman was now assured of the leading spot for Horse of the Year going into the National. The rest of the horses on the circuit would go straight from Washington up to Harrisburg for another week of chances at the Pennsylvania National. Only Snowman would miss the show, returning home to the de Ley-ers and the lessons at Knox.

When Dave Kelley called St. James long-distance that night, the de Leyer clan, clustered near the phone, waiting for news, let out whoops of delight. Winner of the stakes and reserve cham-pion of the show? At the Washington International?

If only they had been able to go along to cheer Snowy on!

Harry was too excited to sleep. He remembered the honor of parading in front of the queen of Holland after the war, on his beloved Petra. Now his horse had paraded in front of the president of his new country. He regretted only that he had not been in the armory to share that moment with his big gray companion. That night, Harry vowed to himself that someday he himself would ride for the president on Snowman.

CHAPTER 20

THE DIAMOND JUBILEE, PART I: OFF TO THE RACES

NEW YORK CITY, NOVEMBER 1958

In New York City, you could always tell when it was time for the National Horse Show. In the first week of November, the *Herald Tribune* devoted half-page spreads to photographs of men in black tie and women wearing evening gowns. Newspaper society columns reported on all the parties and fancy dinners. But this year, the excitement was ratcheted up an extra notch. For this was no ordinary year at the National Horse Show. This was the seventy-fifth year, the Diamond Jubilee.

The National truly was a national event. Competitors came from all over America and from many different countries for a chance to compete in the foremost equestrian competition of the year.

After a grueling summer and fall of competing, it was time for the horse show that tested the strength and stamina of the best of them. This was more than a display of skill or breeding—though both were important. This contest would become a test of spirit—of the quality horsemen call "bottom" and spectators instinctively recognize as heart.

It was the crowning event of every rider's calendar. Everyone in the horse world whom Harry knew would be there. All the professionals he admired and who had mentored him—like Mickey Walsh and Dave Kelley—as well as his toughest competitors, like Adolph Mogavero and Al Fiore.

The show lasted eight days, always opening on Election Day, a Tuesday. There were daytime events and nighttime events. Only the top horses would be selected to perform in the evenings.

Harry was itching to get back into the ring on Snowman. Back in October, he had been forced to sit at home, getting news from the shows at Washington only secondhand. But that was over. What mattered now was that Harry and Snowman had a rare bit of time off and were registered in the National Horse Show. The National had its own magic. Every horseman believed in it. Unexpected things happened. New champions were born in one thundering round under the New York spotlights.

The Garden—Madison Square Garden. Harry remembered the year before, his improbable fourth-place ribbon with Sinjon, and the pain of leaving the horse behind.

Ach, no use in thinking about that.

Coming into the show, everyone thought First Chance would be the horse to beat. No one was thinking about Snowman, who had sat out the Pennsylvania National, the second-biggest show of the year. Harry aimed to prove everyone wrong.

*   *   *

On the morning of November 2, 1958, Harry awoke at three A.M. after having barely slept. He had been out at the barn late, getting the horses ready. Now he had to prepare for the trip to Manhattan. Long before dawn, he tossed fresh hay into Snowman's feeder, straightened his blanket, and gathered up the rolls of wool flannel that he used to bandage the horse's legs to protect them from injury in the horse trailer. The ride into the city—with its jarring potholes and starts and stops—would be harder on a horse than the usual journeys over country roads.

Snowy stood still while Harry crouched beside him, the stall illuminated only by a single bulb. It was cold, and Harry's fingers were stiff but deft. He'd done these preparations hundreds of times before.

The horse must have sensed that something special was about to happen, based on all the bustle of preparation in the predawn light. But he stood patiently as always, munching on hay, while Harry bandaged him. The barn was quiet except for the rustling of the horses in the other stalls and the sound of Harry's dogs sniffing around outside.

Harry looked at his deeply callused hands. They were already gnarled like an old man's, with a couple of broken fingers. These same hands had doctored the gray's wounds, and carried hay for him and measured grain. These hands had groomed the horse and saddled him, rubbed liniment into his legs and iced him through the night when he got hurt.

Each time he set out to ride in a show, he reminded himself that he knew this horse as well as he knew his own children. He had tended to him in sickness and in health as he did his own family. He had ridden the horse in shows but also down to the beach and over the hunting fields. He had watched him carry students and his kids. Other owners did not do that. Other riders had helpers do the dirty work for them. But Harry did not wish that life for himself. That deep-down understanding—that bond between him and his horse—was about much more than winning ribbons. Harry believed it was his secret weapon.

It was still dark as Harry pulled onto Moriches Road, and the neighboring farms were quiet. The children were still asleep; they would come later with Johanna to watch. In the trailer alongside Snowman was the nervous but talented mare, Night Arrest. They would both be competing in the show.

Driving into the city took several hours. Country roads in Suffolk County turned into highways in Nassau County, and then the skyline rose up in front of him. Two hours after leaving the peaceful hamlet of St. James, Harry drove the horse van across Forty-Ninth Street and up Eighth Avenue, the skyscrapers of Manhattan towering overhead. Car horns honked and yellow taxis sped by, cutting in and out of traffic.

They had entered a whole different world.

Other horse trailers were also pulling up along Seventh Avenue. Harry caught his breath, overwhelmed by the busy atmosphere.

As he, Snowy, and Night Arrest made their way into Madison Square Garden, they noticed swarming crowds and groups of reporters getting ready to go inside. An unmistakable aura of grandeur buzzed in the air.

For all the glory upstairs in Madison Square Garden, the basement was a sorry excuse for a stabling area. The ventilation was poor; the air was dusty. Horses could easily catch respiratory infections, which spread like wildfire in the enclosed space. To allow a horse to stretch his legs, you had to walk him up on the street. But as hot and stuffy as it was in the basement, the air outside in the streets of Manhattan was cold—and the contrast could stiffen muscles and make a horse's cold grow worse.

Like everything at the Garden, there was a hierarchy. The best stabling, the best boxes, the best parties, the best order to ride in the competitions, were all distributed to those with social standing and status. Not to people like Harry. Snowman and Night Arrest were given stalls in an out-of-the-way corner, the worst location of all. But Harry never let himself be bothered by small slights. He got started right away, making the horses comfortable. Since Harry was wearing a worker's coveralls instead of fancy riding clothing, wealthy horse owners walking by mistook him for one of the hired hands, never imagining that this dusty-looking groom would soon be competing against them in front of a huge crowd.

The children had made a sign with Snowman's name on it, and Harry tacked it on Snowman's stall door with pride. Johanna and Harriet had pinned up all of Snowman's ribbons next to his stall—an impressive display. But Harry was not trying to try to impress people. He cared about one test, the only one that mattered: the one upstairs in the ring.

People were curious about the gray gelding. His story had been splashed across the papers over the last few days. For New Yorkers riding the subway and reading the paper folded to the sports page, Snowman was a favorite to watch. Spectators came by to get a peek at the horse, admiring the ribbons and the friendly manner in which Snowman greeted everyone. He never seemed to mind a pat on the nose from the passing fans, and Harry didn't mind, either. The whole family smiled and said hello, and the horse seemed to bask in the attention.

Hotheaded Night Arrest was a different story. The unfamiliar, sooty city air and clanging sounds of Seventh Avenue made her skittish and anxious. She was restless in her stall, even with Snowy's calming presence next door. When Harry took her out for exercise in the cramped warm-up area, he had his hands full. He had no idea how Night Arrest would react to the spectacle upstairs, but this was not a good sign.

CHAPTER 21

THE DIAMOND JUBILEE, PART II: A WHOLE NEW WORLD

Nothing said New York City glamour like the National Horse Show. All around was the din and blare of midtown Manhattan, with honking horns, ambulances in the distance, and people everywhere—laughing, talking, and shouting. It was unlike anything the de Leyer children had ever seen.

Through the doors into the grand lobby, one entered another world. Socialites milled around, wearing outfits more befitting a society ball than a venue best known for hosting the Barnum & Bailey Circus. Beautiful people emerged from chauffeured Rolls-Royces. Everyone admired the glitz and glitter of the Latin American teams, whose gold-braided white military jackets and charging riding styles always jazzed up the international events. Even the ticket collectors wore tuxedos.

The press was always out in full force—society and fashion reporters as well as sports columnists came to cover the show for New York's newspapers.

The first tier of seats were the ringside boxes. Around the promenade, hot dog vendors, program salesmen, and souvenir vendors tried to catch the attention of the ordinary folk who passed by the ringside boxes on their way to the cheap seats, known as "heaven," up under the eaves.

Families clutching programs purchased for an expensive $1.50 sat high up above the ring with a good view of the show. Inside the pages of the program were pictures of the trophies to be won, and lists of members of the international teams, plus all the classes and participants.

For kids up in the stands, it was like a wonderland. Even for the de Leyer children—who had grown used to watching their father perform in the horse show ring—the crowds, the spectacle, and the spotlights of Madison Square Garden made the entire experience seem new. As always, they were dressed up under Johanna's watchful eye, but for the next eight nights, they would be allowed to stay up late in the stands and watch. This was the most exciting week of their lives.

The opening ceremonies started at eleven o'clock sharp. Eager to watch the opening ceremonies, crowds packed the stands. Everyone grew more excited as the U.S. Army Marching Band began to play. Unlike the prim, country club crowds at places like Piping Rock, this was mostly a New York crowd, clapping, stomping, cheering, and catcalling as they saw fit. They were noisy and boisterous, whooping from the stands.

Johanna was far too strict to allow her children to join in the mayhem of the crowd, but they sat quietly on the edges of their seats, drinking in every sight and sound of the thrilling spectacle. At ringside, in the press box, the reporters Marie Lafrenz and Alice Higgins, of *Sports Illustrated*, jockeyed for space as they rat-a-tatted away on their manual typewriters.

The international teams paraded in, each stopping in the

center of the arena as the Army Marching Band played its country's national anthem. Every time he saw the parade of nations, Harry could not help but feel some mixed emotions: sadness that his native country of Holland was not represented, and pride in the team of his adopted homeland, the United States of America. He was also tinged with just a shadow of sadness that as a professional, he would never be able to carry his adopted homeland's flag into the ring.

As the program continued, the rowdy crowd gradually settled down. The ringmaster, Honey Craven, wore a royal red waistcoat and a gray silk top hat, modeled in the style of the English Royal Guard. Each class was announced by the call of a long brass English hunting horn. The clear piping on the horn brought every competitor to full attention.

Snowman's first test would be a rematch against Diamant in a fault-and-out class. Fault-and-outs combined timed courses with big spreads—and they always bedeviled the big gray. Harry knew that Diamant, the taller horse, excelled at this kind of class.

Of course, Miss Sears was watching Diamant from her usual private box along the promenade. Her horses had been winning at the Garden for decades. Snowman, on the other hand, was here on his first improbable trip. Who would have guessed that the gray plow horse, a horse auction reject, would be playing against the cream of the crop of the show world?

Horses and riders milled around, unsure when they would be called. Even the most seasoned competitors looked tense. Horses jigged in place, chomping on their bits. The air vibrated with coiled energy just waiting to be released.

Diamant went early. True to form, the athletic horse took

no notice of the lights or the crowd. He zipped through the course with no faults, finishing with an impressively fast time. Harry couldn't help being impressed. To beat Diamant, Snowman would need to cut the course's tight corners even tighter.

Finally, it was their turn. Harry sat astride Snowman, trying to block out the frantic energy around him. He visualized the course in his mind's eye, imagining each turn. Show jumping resembles sports like diving and ice-skating. Years of training and endurance come together in just a few brief, high-risk moments in the spotlight. Every move must be so ingrained, so practiced, so much like breathing that no thought is necessary.

Now it was Harry and Snowman's moment.

The big gates swung open, revealing the ring, the crowds, the flags, and the huge fences.

Harry whispered a word of encouragement and saw Snowy's ear flick back. He patted his neck and urged him forward. In a flash, the Flying Dutchman and his plow horse were lit up in the glaring center-stage lights of Madison Square Garden.

Harry sensed Snowman's mood, reading the horse's signals through his seat bones, thighs, calves, and hands. He kept the reins loose, communicating trust to his horse. Another pat on the neck, then a cluck. Snowman picked up a canter and Harry rose up out of the saddle, leaning forward. "Go, boy, go," he whispered. Noise bounced from the walls of the cavernous Garden, but again, Harry saw an ear flick back. The horse was still listening.

Then all was flying color and spinning motion. The pair flew around the tight turns of the course. Before they knew it, they were heading toward the last fence, a big spread. Harry felt the horse's gathering approach. He measured the length of his stride. The horse elongated his neck. A striped pattern of light from the spotlights fell across the approach, making the distance hard to judge. On the takeoff, Harry sensed a slight miscue. Sure enough, the horse rapped the fence hard with a hind leg.

The pole teetered. Then fell.

The crowd groaned.

Harry dropped his reins and leaned over to pat Snowy with both hands. Snowman had failed to beat Diamant's clear round. Eleo Sears's horse would win first place in this round.

In the winner's circle in the center of the ring, cameras flashed, lighting up the winking silver trophy. Miss Sears accepted it with a gallant air, her weathered, angular face a familiar sight in the ring. When Harry's name was called, he took the red ribbon and waved to the crowd. Second place for the fault-and-out class at the National Horse Show—so what if it wasn't first? They had only just begun. The Diamond Jubilee was already off to a good start.

Next to Snowman's stall, the children added the silken red ribbon. They were certain that Snowman would win first place in the next class.

Nobody could convince them that their horse deserved anything less than the blue.

The next night was the first of the open jumping classes. Any touch or rub against a fence counted against a horse. Diamant did not compete in these classes, but the competition would still be tough. The morning elimination round had already winnowed down the pack. Only the top contenders would jump in the nighttime round. One false step could put a champion out of the running.

Harry was riding both Night Arrest and Snowman tonight. Night Arrest was still worrying him. The mare was fidgety and could not seem to get used to the surroundings. Harry took her to the tiny training area, wedged between the ramp to the arena gate and the edge of the stalls.

Harry rode Night Arrest around the cramped schooling space, trying to calm her. If she was already this nervous in the schooling area, Harry wondered, how would she react to the grand spectacle in the ring? But he didn't have time to think about it any longer. It was their turn. Night Arrest jigged up the ramp, barely contained under Harry's steadying hands. Up at the gate, there was nowhere to circle, just a narrow alleyway. He tried to keep her moving. She was nervous and skittish. Each time the crowd burst out into raucous applause, she spooked and pranced in place.

When the big gate swung open, she shot through it like a stone from a catapult. Harry squeezed the reins and settled his weight deeper in the saddle. But she wasn't listening. As he headed toward the first fence, Harry knew he had his work cut out for him. She made it over the first few fences without mishap, but as he cantered toward the big oxer—a post-and-rail spread fence—she started to come apart. Right before the jump, she threw in an extra stride, leaving her off-kilter on the takeoff.

Before the horse even left the ground, Harry knew she would not be able to clear the hurdle. He braced himself. Night Arrest's front feet flew through the barrier, crashing in a tangle of flying poles. On the landing, she stumbled, about to fall. Harry let his body go soft; he knew it was better to get thrown off a horse than to risk staying on a horse who might tumble on top of him.

But in a disastrous turn of events, his foot caught in the stirrup.

The crowd groaned in horror. The Flying Dutchman pounded across the ring, one stride, two, three, dragged by his hooked foot. People watched the disaster in hushed silence. A minute more and he would be flung against the wooden barrier at the side of the ring. Or, worse yet, kicked in the head. But not a split second too soon, Harry managed to wrench himself free. In a flash, he stood up and patted the dirt from his breeches.

Night Arrest, her sides heaving, stood near the arena wall, trumpeting hot breath through her nose, her eyes still flashing with fear. Harry held out his hand, then slowly walked toward her. She snorted twice, then lowered her head to his outstretched hand. Harry reached up with his other hand. He grasped the reins. She didn't back away. The crowd clapped as the pair left the ring. This brave young man was still standing! Probably only Johanna, up in the stands, could see the way Harry winced when he walked. Harry rarely showed pain. And there was no time to sit and nurse his wounds. He still had Snowman to ride.

As if to taunt him, only two horses took their turns before the gate master called out, "Harry de Leyer on Snowman is in the hole."

Time to get on the big gray.

Putting his bruises out of his mind, Harry stuck a foot

through the stirrup and swung up onto Snowman's back, settling into the saddle. Snowman walked willingly up the ramp, his reins loose. He stood quietly at the in-gate.

The crowd clapped as the pair entered the ring, impressed that the young man was back on another horse so soon. He looked confident enough, even though the crowd had watched him being dragged across the dirt just minutes before.

As always, Harry gave Snowman a chance to pause and survey the crowd. The people in the stands—from the boxes to the cheap seats—cheered and stomped in appreciation. Maybe it was the horse's story that had drawn them in, or maybe it was seeing the young man get up from his dreadful fall, but Harry felt that the crowd was behind him. Harry forced his mind to go blank as he tuned in to his horse. Then there was nothing, no sound, just the feeling of talking to Snowman without words and the sense that he was guiding him around the course with his thoughts alone.

But with only two fences remaining, Harry heard the hollow knock of a hoof hitting the pole. One half fault for a hind touch. Horse and man galloped toward the final fence. If they could clear the last fence with no faults, they'd still be in the running. Snowman sank back, then leapt upward. But Snowman's rear foot knocked the pole from the fence.

Two faults.

A good round . . . but not good enough. Adolph Mogavero took home the blue for Oak Ridge with the flashy mare First Chance. Mogavero, a former jockey and steeplechase rider, had been winning on the show circuit for ten years.

For the first time any of the de Leyers could remember, there was no new ribbon to pin up next to Snowman's stall.

After a season of amazing consistency, Harry and Snowman could not seem to hit their stride.

The children looked crestfallen, but Harry tried to reassure them.

The National Horse Show has many days left! he reminded them. There'd be many more chances.

He went about his barn tasks with the same degree of vigor as usual that night, not telling anyone of the pain and bruises all over his back where he'd fallen. He spent an extra minute in Snowman's stall, whispering encouragement to the big gray.

It was a slow start, but they weren't licked yet. There was still time to be a champion.

CHAPTER 22

THE DIAMOND JUBILEE, PART III: SNOWMAN SOARS

The next day, suddenly, Snowman hit his stride. He flew around his courses with an effortless clean round—securing a spot in the jump-off against First Chance. First Chance had an advantage: Only seven years old, she had spent her entire life as a pampered show horse. Snowman looked like a grizzled veteran in comparison—even though this was the older horse's first outing at the National.

First Chance would be up first. Adolph Mogavero and Harry waited side by side in the narrow alley adjacent to the in-gate. From their vantage point, neither rider could see the fences. As the in-gate swung open, bringing with it the musty smell of the dirt surface of the ring, Harry caught a glance of the shortened, raised course.

The gate man ushered Mogavero and First Chance into the ring, then closed the gate behind them. Harry could not watch Mogavero's ride, but he followed the progress from the sounds: the galloping strides, the brief moment of silence over the fences, the applause that followed each clean fence. A moment later, the gate swung open again. First Chance had put in a clean round.

It was Snowman's turn. Harry turned to acknowledge the crowd, allowing his horse to do the same. Then they got down to business. Harry steadied Snowman on the approach to the first fence. After that, they were perfectly in sync. His body became his horse's body; his soul became his horse's soul.

In a flash, the round was over. Snowman was clean. Another round of fence raising for a second jump-off. The crowd exploded in applause.

As the crew raised the fences, Harry and Adolph Mogavero waited in the wings. Their two horses could not have looked more different. First Chance, naturally high-strung and now more keyed up than ever, jigged in place, then paced in the narrow space. Snowman stood on a loose rein, one leg cocked in a horse's typical resting pose, his ears relaxed to the sides.

Harry held the rein on the buckle. When the gate swung open, First Chance bolted into the ring, leaving a small eddy of wind behind her. Again, Harry listened. This time, he heard the wooden thump of a pole hitting the ground, followed by a small groan from the crowd. The gate swung open as First Chance and Adolph returned. Adolph nodded with a friendly camaraderie.

If First Chance had made an error . . . that meant Snowman had an opening to win. A clean round would bring them the blue ribbon. How many clean rounds had Snowman put in over the last few months? Too many to count. But this was the Garden—not a time to count on anything. As Harry trotted Snowman into the arena, and as the horse turned to look at the stands, the crowd erupted in applause.

There was no time to pay attention to the sights and sounds. Horse and rider had to muster all their concentration, all their training and skill, courage and heart. Twelve challenging fences, twelve chances to fault. In the high-stakes Garden classes, horses faced the highest fences late at night, when they were tired and frazzled and would normally be home in their stalls. More than once, a challenging late-night jump-off had pushed a horse past his limit. The ringmaster and the judge stood by, ready to take note of any mistake.

Back in St. James, by this time of night, Snowman would have been hanging his head over his stall door, his belly full of hay, looking at the stars in the dark countryside sky. Instead, the gray horse was about to face a difficult and highly demanding challenge.

Harry gathered up the reins and squeezed his horse around the barrel with his calves. He whispered a word of encouragement. Now or never.

Snowman stretched his neck out and bounded toward the fences with an evident joy. Up in the stands, the crowd seemed to be entranced as he soared over each fence. It was as if the horse was freed from the pull of gravity, freed from his past and from the plow that had once weighed him down. Twelve times he flew, clearing the fences with room to spare. Twelve perfect fences. No faults. For the first time, the blue ribbon at the National Horse Show belonged to the big gray gelding, the lesson horse from the Knox School.

Returning to the center of the ring to receive his prize, Snowman ambled along behind Harry, seemingly unaware of the ruckus that surrounded his victory. Up in the stands, thousands of people—families with children, shopkeepers, police officers, secretaries—looked down from "heaven," their perch high up in cheap seats close to the Garden's high ceiling, clapping wildly and cheering uproariously, smitten by the horse who seemed to fly without wings. This horse knew how to steal hearts. That he had already stolen the heart of the handsome young man who rode him was apparent for all to see. Harry led the horse around the arena for a victory lap. The affection between the two could not be missed.

That night, the de Leyers hung a blue ribbon next to their horse's stall. For the first time, a little bit of that Garden magic settled over their corner of their stables.

But the show was hardly over. The open jumper competition was not one contest but a *series* of contests. Each day brought a new series of grueling jump-offs and tiring courses. Opportunities for mistakes were everywhere. The courses demanded that the horses perform flawlessly, time after time. The following day, First Chance pulled ahead again, beating out Snowman.

And now, the two horses were neck and neck for the championship. The competition was fierce. Every horse in the show had talent—but stamina would win in the end.

Up in heaven, munching on hot dogs doused in mustard, the ordinary folk held their breath, spellbound, every time Harry trotted into the ring. Harry smiled and waved to them after each clean round, raising his eyes up above the boxes to take in the entire crowd, and Snowman always followed suit.

For Harry, the week passed in a blur. Caring for the horses and keeping them in show shape in the cramped basement of the Garden was almost a round-the-clock affair. The jumper classes sometimes did not start until ten at night. The jump-offs could stretch until one or two in the morning. After each class, Harry had to get the horses hot-walked and rubbed down, fed and groomed, and then the routine started up again in the predawn hours.

The week that at first had seemed as if it would last forever was suddenly drawing to a close. The show's last day would feature the open jumper stakes. To earn the accolade Triple Crown, a horse would first have to win three different prizes: the American Horse Shows Association (AHSA) Horse of the Year, the PHA Championship, and the National Horse Show Championship. The AHSA Horse of the Year and PHA honors were decided on points accumulated throughout the season, and Snowman had already earned enough points to secure those two prizes.

Going into the last night of the National, the final leg of the Triple Crown was at stake. If Snowman won the class, he would make a clean sweep, winning show jumping's top three honors.

The last class of the show involved two rounds—one in the afternoon, and one that night. Points for the two rounds would be added together to decide the champion. The only horses still in contention for show champion were Snowman and First Chance—with First Chance at a one-point lead.

CHAPTER 23

UNDER THE SPOTLIGHTS

NEW YORK CITY, NOVEMBER 1958

On the eve of the last night of the show, Marie Lafrenz, who had been reporting on the show for the *Herald Tribune*, came to Harry with an idea. Lafrenz didn't pitch stories to newspapers only; she had seen the power of television. But she knew that to get a horse story on the air, she needed to have an extraordinary tale to tell. So she pitched the story of the winning plow horse to a popular talk show on NBC: *The Tonight Show*. The usual host was Jack Paar, but tonight, a young man named Johnny Carson would be the guest host.

Harry hesitated. How was he supposed to get his horse to the NBC television studios when he had a class coming up that night? Then an idea popped into his head. If it wasn't too far, perhaps he could just walk. Harry, leading Snowman, and Marie Lafrenz walked east to the NBC studios in Rockefeller Plaza at Sixth Avenue and Forty-Ninth Street, passing through the Broadway theater district en route. Snowman ambled along amid the noise and confusion of midtown, much to the delight of nearby pedestrians and cabbies, who leaned out of their yellow taxis to shout encouragement.

In the *Tonight Show* studio, Harry and Snowman found themselves plunged into an unfamiliar world. The show was filmed on a soundstage. The backdrop, with Carson's desk and the chairs for his guests, was lit up by big, hot lights. The cameramen, wearing headphones, sat behind huge, newfangled-looking television cameras. A microphone moved around on a long wire suspended above the stage, accidentally dipping into the picture from time to time.

Beyond the lit-up stage, a live studio audience sat in the small theater. The space was hardly suited for an animal. Certainly not a show horse. The studio was noisy, crowded with technicians and complicated electronics. To a man like Harry, the scene looked almost spooky, like something from the future.

Snowman waited in the wings until it was his time to appear onstage. Smiling at the camera, Johnny Carson retold the story of the eighty-dollar wonder horse. Then Snowman, led by Harry, stepped out onto the cramped stage, looking around, calm as usual, his big, sleepy eyes blinking at the hot, bright lights. Harry reassured the TV host that the horse was gentle. Right there, on the tiny stage, Johnny Carson climbed up a stepladder onto Snowman's back, sitting backward, facing the horse's tail. Harry held on to Snowman's halter, but the horse went along with the stunt, seeming to almost smile at the camera. The audience erupted in delighted laughter and applause.

Harry did not realize it, but in those few minutes, the horse's fame spread far beyond the Garden and New York City. People were only beginning to understand the power of television. When Snowman walked back to Eighth Avenue and

Top: Harry and Snowman in the field near the stable on a winter day.

Right: Harry and Snowman out riding. Snowman proved to be a quiet and steady mount.

JACKIE BITTNER, *President*
Left to Right: Evelyn Schulz, Kitsie Chambers, Jackie Bittner, Ann Mead, Wendy Plumb.

Harry de Leyer

Knox School Riding Club

The Knox School Riding Club.

Riding lessons in the courtyard of the horseshoe-shaped stable at the Knox School.

Knox girls in their camel hair coats standing near the Knox School limousine.

Top: Harry (front, right) carries the flag of St. Oedenrode in the parade to celebrate the queen of Holland's return from exile in 1945.

Right: Harry's father astride his horse. The church in St. Oedenrode is in the background.

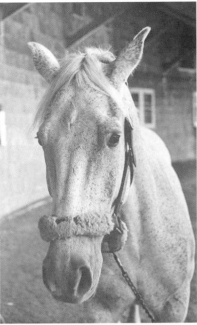

Left: Trainer Cappy Smith was known for his acumen about horses and his movie-star good looks.

Right: Snowman was a "man's best friend" kind of horse.

The former paddock jumper excelled at high vertical fences, snapping his knees up tight to clear each obstacle.

Harry trained Snowman to jump on a loose rein. Here he lets go of the reins, trusting his horse with total freedom.

Left: Harry and Snowman share a moment of affection.

Bottom: Harry sits astride his flea-bitten gray with the calm of a prince.

Left: Harry drops the reins over the fence, to the amazement of the crowd.

Bottom: Entering the winner's circle, Harry often brought one of the kids along for the ride.

The glamour boys of the United States Equestrian Team fresh from a winning season in Europe. (Left to right) Frank Chapot, George Morris, Hugh Wiley, and Bill Steinkraus.

Bill Steinkraus riding Eleonora Sears's champion jumper Ksar d'Esprit.

Frank Chapot riding Eleonora Sears's expensive German import, Diamant.

In a tackroom in the basement stables, a competitor looks over his equipment before his class begins. Outside the tackroom, a groom is preparing his horse for the competition.

Left: The Royal Canadian Mounted Police parade through the arena at Madison Square Garden while the audience, in evening wear, watches from the sidelines.

Right: A nattily-turned-out competitor parades through the ring in a *Life* magazine article about the National Horse Show.

Willard Mullin's cartoon about Snowman's rags-to-riches story appeared in the
World-Telegram and Sun on the eve of the 1958 National Horse Show.

Left: Turned loose in the ring, Snowman jumped fences just for the fun of it.

Bottom: (Left to right) Joseph (Chef), Harriet, and Marty riding Snowman in Long Island Sound.

Right: At an exhibition, Snowman jumps over Lady Gray. Harry is in the saddle, and Chef is holding Lady Gray.

Bottom: All aboard: the de Leyer family saddled up near Branglebrink Farms. (Left to right) Harry riding Snowman, Johanna on Lady Gray, Chef, Harriet, Marty, Billy, Harry junior, and Andre.

Top: Snowman at a book signing in Stony Brook, New York.

Left: Busloads of schoolchildren used to come to Hollandia Farms to visit Snowman.

Forty-Ninth Street, to the basement stables, he and his young rider had been transformed into celebrities.

Snowman had been performing well, throwing himself into every event, but it had been a long, grueling week. He was holding steady in second place, though First Chance still had that one-point lead. And the show horses' audience had grown, so the pressure was really on. Television viewers across the country were now tuned in to the outcome of this contest at Madison Square Garden.

The top twelve horses from the last day's afternoon event were invited to compete in a great stakes class—the last contest before the closing ceremonies. This was a championship class. The fences were higher and the spreads greater than they had ever been.

Before the class, Harry gathered Johanna and the kids together. "Keep your clothes nice and don't muss them up," he told them. "If we win, we'll all go out together."

Harry was down in the basement doing last-minute preparations—checking his stirrup leathers and irons, tucking the leather keepers into place on Snowman's bridle, adjusting the horse's crownpiece and throat latch.

He took a deep breath, swung into the saddle, and rode Snowman up the ramp to the in-gate. Tonight, Harry was not representing any one particular nation—he was representing the little guy. He was riding for anyone who had ever been kicked around or neglected or underestimated. Anyone who had ever been shoved to the margins, given up on, or rendered invisible. The special bond between Harry and Snowman was the bond of survivors. Here was a horse so beat-up that nobody thought his life was worth saving, and here was a man who, his life destroyed by war, had had to start fresh in a country where he did not speak the language and had no capital except that of his own two hands, his love for his family, and his personal dignity.

Tonight, Harry wanted to *win*—for Snowman, for his American family, for his Dutch family, for himself. This was the biggest night of the biggest horse show of Harry de Leyer's life. The big plow horse had captivated all who had seen him, but that guaranteed nothing.

Twelve horses, twelve riders, twelve owners: a year of training, discipline, and sacrifices to get ready for this one night. Nerves had no place. Fatigue was no excuse. This was a time for a rider to dig deep, to ask of his horse, and to see what the horse had left to give back. The last night of the last week of the last show of the year. Tonight, this was a test of courage—of heart.

Harry sat astride his old Teddy Bear, reins loose, the same look of unflappable calm on his face that the spectators had seen there all week. Nobody at the show except Johanna knew about the time that Harry, as a boy, had driven a beer wagon past Nazi checkpoints with contraband grain hidden inside one of the empty kegs. Nobody knew about the time he had found his brother Jan lying as still as a stone in the field after touching a cultivator made live by a blown-down electric wire. Nobody knew that Harry de Leyer—had World War II not intervened—would probably be on the Dutch team, riding the European circuit, getting the best horses, and looking toward a berth for the 1960 Olympics. You could not read any of that on Harry's face—but you could not miss the look of steadiness.

It was something shared by man and horse. These two understood the meaning of endurance. Both knew you could do no better than to give it your all.

As the riders and horses circled the schooling area, as grooms scurried about flicking away invisible bits of dust from their charges, Harry and Snowman seemed above the fray. The horse was relaxed, and so was the man. They would help each other, come what may. So far, not a single horse had achieved a clean round. Any faults and the horses would enter a grueling jump-off, but a clean round would win the title.

The big gates swung open and Snowman entered the ring. As usual, Harry gave him a moment to survey the crowd. The sounds of the shouting and applause from up in the cheap seats was deafening. Harry tipped his hat to acknowledge the support. Then the noise, the people, and even the grand hall itself all fell away.

There was nothing left but the sound of his horse's footsteps on the dirt, the line to the next fence, the gathering, the lift, the soar. Each approach to each fence was fluid, each takeoff sure, each landing effortless. Harry and Snowman seemed in such harmony that it was hard to tell where one stopped and the other began. Harry guided the horse through the tight turns, over the crossbars and hanging gate, the brush box and the big wall. Each fence seemed effortless; the horse appeared to float in midair, leaving room to spare.

When Snowman soared over the final fence, Harry dropped the reins and raised his arms in an exuberant hurrah. As Snowman galloped calmly over the finish, he grabbed the horse around the neck and kissed him.

Not until they were finished did he hear the crowd cheering

and shouting. Because they had done it. They had won! There were no challengers.

Snowman had clinched the championship.

Down in the stables, Johanna and the children were waiting. Johanna looked lovely in a dark blue suit with fur trim. The boys had on blue jackets and bow ties, and Harriet wore a button-up party dress with a flounce.

The children were young, the arena was large, and the crowd was noisy and quite frightening, but the family followed their beloved Snowman up the steep ramp, through the big white gates, and into the ring. When the crowd saw the de Leyer family, with the children lining up in stair-step fashion, they went even wilder than before.

It was a clean sweep. The National Horse Show Triple Crown. Snowman was Horse of the Year, the PHA Champion, *and* the Champion of Madison Square Garden's Diamond Jubilee. It was an honor that all the other owners, with all their money, could not buy. And Snowman was presented with a snow-white cooler, a big, thick woolen blanket that covered his neck to his haunches and hung down to his knees. The cooler had 1958 CHAMPION emblazoned on the side. From now on, whenever Snowman went to a show, he could parade around the grounds wearing that cooler.

Flashbulbs popped as newsmen snapped picture after picture of the champion horse and the de Leyer family. Harry had the big engraved silver tray in his hand. Behind him stood the beloved gray horse.

Harry did not realize it then, but from that day forward,

things would never be the same. That horse, whose picture was splashed all over newspapers the next day, who had been seen on television—now it was more than just Harry's children who loved him, and the girls at Knox, and the people lucky enough to be up in the stands. Snowman was the people's horse.

Every child who saw the horse's proud parade under the spotlights went home inspired. On that November night in 1958, it started to seem as though anything was possible.

CHAPTER 24

FAMOUS!

NEW YORK CITY, 1958

No one truly knows how he or she will respond if struck by the blinding light of fame, unless it happens to them. Harry de Leyer arrived at Madison Square Garden in 1958 as an unknown and an underdog. But in one glorious, blinding week at the Garden, all that changed.

At the end of the horse show—after the jumper stakes, after the family paraded under the spotlights, after the trophies were awarded and the photos snapped and sent out over the wires—that's when the real business of the horse show began.

After the big win, the stable was abuzz with well-wishers and newspapermen, new fans and old rivals, who had come to pay their respects.

Snowman. The eighty-dollar wonder horse, the Cinderella horse, as the press was calling him, was the sports world's newest sensation. He had shown under the colors of Hollandia Farms, Harry and Johanna's small family enterprise. But now he was everyone's darling.

Just hours after the big win, while Harry was still dressed in his work clothes with a pitchfork in his hand, an entrepreneur named Bert Firestone came calling. Firestone, who had made a fortune in New York real estate, was also a horseman who had competed during the show in the hunter division.

He approached Harry after the show with an offer: he wanted to buy Snowman. Right then and there. Harry could name his price.

Bert Firestone was a big man with broad shoulders and a round face. He looked Harry in the eye—and saw hesitation.

Harry was thinking. He still remembered leaving the Garden the year before with an empty horse van behind him. He remembered watching Sinjon walk away from him into the shadowy basement stabling.

"Thirty-five thousand dollars," Bert said. "I'll pay for him right now. Take him home with me."

Thirty-five thousand dollars! Enough to buy a new farm outright. Ten times more money than Harry earned in a year.

Harry shook his head. Not for all the money in the world. Not even for life-changing money, like the kind Firestone was talking about. Snowman had earned his place in the family. Harry had promised never to let him go. He had been foolish enough to sell him once. But the horse had known better, and had come back. Harry was not going to make the same mistake twice. Bert had a check in his hand. He held it up for Harry to look at.

"The check is signed. You can fill in the amount."

Bert extended his hand, as though expecting a shake.

Harry shook his head slowly. Even with such an astronomical sum, he knew he did not have to ask Johanna. There are things a person cannot put a price on.

"He's not for sale," Harry said. "My children love him."

Harry saw that Firestone was starting to understand.

The two men shook hands, and as the magnate walked away, leaving Harry to his work, Harry turned and looked at his plow horse without any regrets.

The morning after the win, the newspapers told and retold the story of Snowman's rags-to-riches triumph. Harry and Snowman seemed to capture the pull-yourself-up-by-your-bootstraps approach so many Americans admired.

You would not have known, spending time with the de Leyers, that they now had in their stable one of the best-loved horses in the country. At home, life continued unchanged. As usual, the family did everything together, from barn work and chores to meals and riding. And Snowman, back in his stall at Knox, took up his life as a lesson horse again.

After the Garden, the season went on hiatus through the winter months, but Harry was as busy as ever with the schoolgirls. He kept them riding straight through the depth of winter, bundled up in woolen jackets, heavy scarves, and thick mittens. And when he set them aboard the big gray, Harry raised the jumps a bit higher than they were used to, cheering them on and reminding them to grab Snowy's thick mane for balance.

Life had returned to its usual rhythms. And the family would soon move from the chicken farm into a slightly larger farm on the corner of Edgewood Avenue, a quiet street a bit closer to the center of St. James. The house was smaller, but the barn was a little bigger, with more room for the horses.

As spring drew near, Harry made plans to take Snowman

out on the circuit again—maybe they could even repeat the performance of the year before.

But even if life had returned to normal, signs abounded that things were not *exactly* the same.

At the stable, reporters came around, asking to see the wonder horse. A vitamin company offered Harry's horses a free supply of supplements, and put a picture of Snowman soaring over a fence in an advertisement. Even Hollywood came calling, with fast-talking agents asking to make a star out of Snowman. This horse, they said, belonged in the movies.

The schoolmistresses of the Knox School, who had at first seemed uninterested in the young riding teacher's successes, began to sing a different tune. It seemed that everyone wanted their daughter to train with the man who had won a championship. The phone in the admissions office was ringing off the hook, and the school was establishing a terrific reputation as a wonderful place for horse-minded girls. Harry was happy with his job, and his bosses were happy with him.

Soon it was March, and the show season opened again— and this time it was clear from the start: Snowman was unstoppable. As the drumbeat started building up to the National Horse Show, once again Harry and Snowman held the lead for the Horse of the Year trophy. Once again, spectators lined up to watch his thrilling performances. Now everybody wanted a piece of this horse.

But that summer bad news came from back home in Holland. Harry's mother was suffering from cancer. It was time for the family to make a visit—and in an incredible stroke of good fortune, Snowman was invited to do an overseas tour of exhibitions. Nine years after arriving in the United States as immigrants, Harry and Johanna were bringing the whole family—four-legged and two-legged—for a visit back home.

Snowman rode abroad in style in a specially equipped turbo-prop plane, just like the ones that ferried the Olympic horses to and from Europe. Their departure was filmed by a crew from MGM, which captured the moment when Snowman walked up the ramp to the waiting aircraft.

For the rest of his life, Harry would remember the moment he walked with Snowman and his son Marty across the tarmac in Amsterdam. It had been less than a decade since he and Johanna had left home on the SS *Volendam*, his beloved mare Petra left behind, his hopes and aspirations tucked away with his saddle and boots in the solitary crate that had contained all of their worldly possessions. Striding across the tarmac today, holding Snowman's lead rope in his hand, he was returning a champion.

In St. Oedenrode, the de Leyer farm still looked the same—the high, peaked red roofs and stucco façade, the chickens that pecked in the stable yard, the brewery, and the fields surrounding the farm. Harry's brother Jan, who had made virtually a full recovery from his fall all those years ago, was still riding horses. The brothers were thrilled to see each other. The town was plastered with posters announcing the arrival of the American champion. Harry and Snowman performed true to form, jumping brilliantly in several exhibitions. Snowman now had fans on both sides of the Atlantic.

But the trip was tinged with sadness. The children spent

time with their grandmother, and they all knew that this first visit together would likely be the last. Soon enough, it was time to go back to New York and say goodbye to Europe.

On Election Day, 1959, the de Leyer clan was back at the Garden. This time, they arrived as celebrities. Snowman was here to defend his title as winner. By now, millions of people knew about his humble life as a plow horse, and about the family who loved him.

Down in Hollandia's corner of the basement, not much had changed. Harry still pulled on coveralls to do his stable work. Johanna and the children slipped on wooden shoes and helped out with the chores. And Snowman, as usual, took the whole spectacle of the seventy-sixth annual National Horse Show in stride.

But Snowman was not the only horse in the headlines at the start of this year's competition. Windsor Castle, fresh from the open jumper victory at Harrisburg, was commanding headlines, too.

Windsor Castle was a horse to be reckoned with. He had dominated the competition at Harrisburg that year. Though Snowman was the sentimental favorite, most horsemen thought he had little chance to beat out the younger horse this year. People were already starting to say that Windsor Castle was the most talented horse on the jumping circuit.

In fact, the young horse was in high demand. Many wealthy horse owners were interested in buying him. And his current owners, a couple of horse traders from Chicago, had no qualms about selling him. In the middle of the horse show, his owners sold him for the astronomical sum of $50,000. "We have no sentimental attachment toward the horse," one of them said about Windsor Castle. "It's business."

There was one thing the de Leyer family made clear: their horse might be beating the high-priced competition in show jumping's competitive stratosphere, but this was *not just* business. Down in their musty corner of the stable, the de Leyer family showed their love to Snowman, taking extra care with his grooming, keeping bits of carrot in their pockets, and scratching his favorite spot on his neck to make him laugh. Other owners never seemed to think about how their horses might feel, moving from one owner to the next without the slightest regard—but for Snowman, it was different. Snowman might have been a jumping champion, but he was a member of the de Leyer family, no matter how valuable he became.

Throughout the eight days, Snowman and Windsor Castle traded places with winning. The horses' points were close. The last class of the show, the $5,000 championship stakes, was the biggest prize Harry had ever competed for. In 1959, $5,000 was the average American annual salary! Harry pushed the thought of the big check out of his mind as he and Snowman waited for their turn; he concentrated only on his horse and on the task at hand.

Snowy's entry into the arena was greeted with a roar. Harry waved to his fans, grinning broadly, then headed for the first fence. In a brilliant whirl, Snowman and Harry put in a seemingly effortless clear round, cinching the big purse and the tricolor. That final victory clinched Snowman's place: the big gray was the first horse in history to win the PHA *and* AHSA Horse of the Year honors two years in a row. None of the other horses—not Diamant, not First Chance, not even Windsor Castle, the $50,000 horse—had matched Snowman's performance in 1959.

For a second year running, Snowy had stolen the show! And just like that, only nine years after landing in Hoboken with his wooden crate and his young bride, the Dutch immigrant had become a household name.

CHAPTER 25

THE WIND OF CHANGE

ST. JAMES, LONG ISLAND, 1960

In January 1960, the British prime minister, Harold Macmillan, gave his famous "Wind of Change" speech, in which he signaled that the long era of British colonialism was coming to an end. Later that year, John F. Kennedy won the Democratic Party's nomination for U.S. president. Change was in the air around the world.

Busy with his duties at Knox, Harry gave little thought to world affairs as the 1960 spring season started to roll into high gear.

Harry was careful not to overjump Snowman. Snowman was healthy and full of life. He still loved to splash around with the de Leyer children on the beaches of Long Island. But at thirteen-odd years old, his legs might not bear up well to the stress of repetitive jumping. Jumping put a lot of wear and tear on a horse, and Snowman had already faced more hard labor than the average horse before he'd even started his career as a jumper.

In the spring and summer, Snowman and Harry went to the familiar round of shows: Fairfield and Lakeville, and the seashore circuit of Sands Point, North Shore, and Piping Rock. Only three years had passed since Snowman had entered his first show as a junior jumper. Show jumping was quickly changing from an insider affair to a big-time sport. There were more horses, more money, more competitions. Wealthy owners were swapping and buying horses for tons of money.

Harry planned to keep going with Snowman as long as the horse still seemed to enjoy it, but not a day longer.

Snowman had won the hearts of horse fans across the whole country. And that meant that now he was held to high expectations. A *Reader's Digest* article titled "The Farm Horse That Became a Champion" brought the horse's story to millions more people. That same year, a Dutch version of the story was published. People no longer came out just to see the plow horse who could jump; they came out to see him win.

The summer season was going well. By the time it wound down, though, Snowman was not in the lead for the prestigious PHA prize. Still, having racked up a string of firsts, seconds, and thirds, he remained among the top contenders.

Whenever Snowman faulted or won the second- or third-place ribbon, Harry saw the look of disappointment clouding the eyes of the children watching from the bleachers. But to Harry, the change in Snowy's performance made sense. After all, the gray horse was getting on in age. As always, he tried his best. Week after week he put in solid performances. It was just that now—when competing against younger, newer horses— sometimes, he was not good enough.

* * *

The summer whirled by in a familiar pattern of horse shows and hamburgers, of rides and ribbons, of trophies and triumphs, and the occasional defeat. Then as the Knox year started up, the de Leyers settled down to their school-year routine. But this year would be different. In October, Harry and Snowman were going to Washington, DC.

Harry knew the competition would be fearsome. Windsor Castle had been cleaning up all over the show circuit, and at this international show, the nine-year-old gelding would surely make a splash. There were newcomers from all over, and some of the old favorites were still going strong. Snowman had triumphed once in Washington with Dave Kelly, but Harry had not been there to see it.

This time, the de Leyers and Snowman were no longer ordinary competitors; they were also special guests, invited to perform an exhibition before the show—their first in front of a crowd of this size. And now, Harry's turn to ride before the president had finally come.

On October 10, 1960, Harry trailered Snowy to Washington with a happy sense of anticipation. Johanna had stayed behind with the younger children, but Chef and Harriet came along to help, along with Jim Troutwell, Harry's buddy and groom.

Chef and Harriet squeezed into the front seat of the van, bouncing in their seats with excitement. Harry drove along the highway with his window rolled down and the radio playing, a hamper of Johanna's famous sandwiches next to him, and his kids playing hooky. Today, they planned to let go of the pressure a little bit. This time, they were going to have some fun.

The grandeur of the opening ceremonies, with the U.S. Army Marching Band and the parade of international teams, always drew a big crowd. In the afternoon, special exhibitions were planned: dancing dressage horses, cowboys on roping horses, and, of course, the world-famous jumper Snowman.

Harry was up next. Head high, he entered the ring aboard Snowman. Horse and rider pulled out all the stops, starting the show by flying over a series of high fences. While arching over them, Harry confidently tossed the reins down. The crowd gasped.

In the wings, Harriet and Chef awaited their turn. It was always fun to see their father show off his skills. But this exhibition was also a time for *them* to be in the spotlight. At home, the sister and brother had been practicing a showstopping trick. And now it was their time to shine.

Chef held on to the lead rope of the second horse they had brought for the occasion, Lady Gray. A flea-bitten gray, like Snowman, she was a sweet lesson horse. In fact, Lady Gray and Snowman looked so much alike that some people had trouble telling them apart, and the two horses were friends.

At the signal from their dad, Chef and Harriet walked into the big arena, leading the gray mare behind them. The jump crew had set up a big square oxer fence, as high as Lady Gray's withers. Harry circled Snowman around and they flew over the fence.

The audience started to murmur. What was going to happen next? they wondered.

Cued by his father, Chef led Lady Gray between the two halves of a spread fence.

Just then, the children heard the spectators gasp as Harry and Snowman bore down on the fence, this time with the other horse standing smack in the way. To clear the hurdle, Snowy would have to clear Lady Gray *and* the fence. Bravely, Chef, nine years old, stood holding Lady Gray's lead rope, watching Snowy approach. One false move would result in a tragic tangle of legs and horseflesh.

There were no false moves. Just as they had practiced, the big horse, his trademark small ears pricked forward, soared over fence and horse with room to spare. It was breathtaking.

The crowd erupted in applause. Chef grinned shyly and fished a carrot out of his pants pocket to feed to Lady Gray. None of them, neither horse, nor child, nor Harry, had ever had even a moment's doubt.

During the nighttime competitions, the armory looked splendid with the tricolored bunting, presidential box, and Army Marching Band. The feel of the show was more cosmopolitan, less stuffy high-society, than the Garden.

The opening event of the evening was the fault-and-out, in which a horse would be eliminated by a single fault. Right away, it became clear that from a huge field of open jumpers, it was going to come down to a contest between the big two: Windsor Castle and Snowman.

The pair of horses were a study in contrasts. Snowman,

the gentle giant, would safely carry a small child or a beginner on his broad back. Brilliant but erratic, Windsor Castle had a firecracker temperament. When the horse was on his game, he could be unbeatable, but other times, he was a dirty stopper, or refused even to let his rider mount.

With every class, the two accomplished horses seemed to be passing the torch of victory back and forth. On the last night of the show, just one class remained: the President's Cup, a new trophy to be awarded for the first time this year. Harry was worried that Snowman was tired. He hoped there would be no jump-off. But again, all the horses were eliminated except the gray and the bay. To settle the score, the announcer declared yet another a jump-off.

It had been a long week, full of competitive jump-offs, and Snowman had given his all. Competing against a younger horse had taken its toll on the big gray.

Snowman stood a chance to win the cup—but it would be challenging. It was late and the fences were high. Harry had half a mind to bow out now, but he knew how much that would disappoint the crowds. After all, they'd turned out chiefly to see Snowman compete.

In the schooling area outside the armory arena, grooms were working over Windsor Castle, rubbing down his haunches with liniment so he wouldn't stiffen up. Windsor Castle's rider, Joe Green, wasn't helping them the way Harry would have. Green stood off to the side in a huddle with the horse's owner, engaged in a whispered conversation. It almost looked as though they were plotting something. Noticing this, Harry furrowed his brow. But he had other things to worry about. Snowman was up first.

Harry entered the ring. He urged Snowman into a canter, leaning forward to give the gelding a pat on the neck. As they galloped toward the big fence, Harry felt the horse's slight reluctance. He tried to silently communicate to the horse that they could manage just fine. The pair rounded the course, gathering for another takeoff.

But Snowman could not quite do it. Over one of the big post-and-rails, his takeoff was simply not strong enough, and as he landed, a pole fell into the dirt with a dull thud. Finishing his round, Harry patted Snowman, loosened his reins, and waved to the crowd as they left the arena. He wasn't too worried. Joe Green's mount might take down a pole or two as well. The class was not over yet.

But when Harry exited the arena, he was surprised by what he saw. Joe Green was standing on the ground next to Windsor Castle. Sitting astride the bay instead was twenty-year-old Kathy Kusner from Virginia. Petite at 4'11", she was an ace rider and one of this year's sensations in the show ring. Not only was she younger than most of the other competitors, she was also female—the only young woman competing in such a grueling event. As far as Harry knew, she had never ridden Windsor Castle before, but now she was poised to ride into the ring for the final class.

What on earth was going on? Harry wondered. A single glance told him the whole story; barely five feet tall, Kusner probably did not weigh a hundred pounds. For a tired horse, taking away the extra forty or fifty pounds by putting a lighter rider in the saddle might make all the difference.

It was a gutsy move to trade out a rider at the last minute—and Harry admired guts. He wished young Kusner luck as he watched her ride into the ring. She might have been small, but Harry had seen enough of her work to know that she was a tough competitor.

Sure enough, the petite dynamo piloted the horse with flair. Windsor Castle finished with a clear round. Harry noticed Joe Green grinning. Clearly, his plan had worked. Windsor Castle won the President's Cup. Kathy Kusner's ride had cinched the deal.

The de Leyers waited anxiously as the judge toted up the scores. To determine the show's champion jumper, they would add up the scores from all the week's events. Windsor Castle and Snowman were neck and neck. Only the show's champion would enter the parade of champions. Only the champion would salute the president of the United States. Would Harry and Snowman get their chance?

At last, the PA system crackled, and Harry felt his heart skip a beat. The children exchanged looks and kept their fingers crossed.

The announcer's deep voice boomed, *Champion jumper of the Washington National Horse Show: Snowman!*

When it was time for the parade of champions, Harry led Snowman into the ring as the U.S. Army Marching Band played, and the crowd cheered uproariously. As they crossed in front of the presidential box, they stopped to salute President Eisenhower, and Harry's heart filled with pride. He and Snowman had reached the moment they had worked toward for so long, and so diligently. The immigrant and his cast-off horse were standing in front of the president of the United States. Harry knew he would remember this moment forever.

CHAPTER 26

CAMELOT

NEW YORK CITY, 1960

November 8, 1960. Election Day. And this was a momentous one. Democrat John F. Kennedy was running against the Republican Richard Nixon. The seventy-seventh National Horse Show opened with its usual pageantry. The de Leyer children lined up in the stands, eyes lit up with excitement. As the two-time reigning champion, their beloved family pet was the star of this year's show.

Harry had told the children not to worry. Snowman would do his best. But, privately, Harry was concerned. All these jump-offs late into the night had taken a toll on the horse. Harry had rested Snowman in the lead-up to the National, hoping to give his horse time to recover. Snowman was such a favorite now, beloved all over America, that Harry had started to think of him as "the people's horse." He knew that Snowman always tried his hardest, and he hated to disappoint his fans, but Harry knew that a fresh posse of horses would be waiting to steal Snowman's national crown.

By the end of that day, John F. Kennedy had been declared the winner of the election. As though in celebration, the first class of the show started beautifully for Snowman, too. He brought home the blue in the first open jumper class.

There seemed to be more wheeling and dealing than ever at the National Horse Show. Big sums of money were changing hands behind the scenes. Harry knew he could sell Snowman in an instant. But word had gotten around that the horse was not for sale. Harry de Leyer was not cut from the usual cloth, and people had figured that out.

When Harry wasn't competing or looking after the horses, he was an avid spectator in the stands. He especially loved to watch the international team competitions. The pageantry of the parades, the different riding styles of the riders from different countries, the playing of the national anthems—it was a chance for Harry to watch and learn from top riders without being involved in the competition. There were teams from Canada, Mexico, France, and the United States, among others.

The sentimental favorite on the American team was the old horse Trail Guide, with Frank Chapot on board. Harry had a soft spot for twenty-one-year-old Trail Guide. That horse was a relic of the old days, when the international team jumping had been a military event.

Here at the Garden, the fences were high, the times were swift, and the competition was intense. The first round for the Good Will Challenge kicked off with a four-way tie—four riders with clean rounds: Frank Chapot, George Morris of the United States, the Canadian, and the Venezuelan. The jump-off started: the Venezuelan knocked down two poles, but Morris had a clean round. The Canadian also put in a clean round, but his time was not as fast. When Trail Guide and Frank Chapot entered the ring, the pressure was on. To win the class, he would have to go clean and fast enough to beat Morris on time.

The brave old horse flew over the first two fences, sailing over them clean. But over the third fence, something went horribly wrong. In the blink of an eye, Trail Guide caught a foot on a rail and fell in a gruesome flipping crash. Harry watched in horror as the horse slid into the side barrier with a sickening thud. As the crowd sat in stunned silence, Frank Chapot got to his feet, unhurt. But the grand old horse lay uncannily still.

From the stands, Harry instantly knew that the situation was bad. The horse show vet, Dr. Joseph O'Dea, rushed into the ring. Used to jumping in to help, Harry followed the doctor. The horse was alive but not moving. When a horse falls and is hurt, he thrashes, his instinct telling him to get to his feet. A horse unable to stand sparks dread in a horseman. There is no more frightening sight than twelve hundred pounds of horseflesh down on the ground, unable to rise. Harry crouched near the horse's head, watching as Dr. O'Dea checked him over in silence. The gelding was perfectly still, moving nothing but his dark brown eyes.

Up in the stands, you could hear a pin drop. The crowd sat in horrified silence. Someone dimmed the lights to the ring. The minutes ticked on, the dark quiet punctuated by the sounds of muffled movement.

Dr. O'Dea worked over the horse. But there was no hope. The valiant old horse would not stand up or walk out of that ring.

In the darkness, as the riders of the equestrian team shed

silent tears, Dr. O'Dea put down the horse. Trail Guide, who had carried the flag of his country, the last horse of the American cavalry, had passed away.

Eventually, the lights came back up and the show went on. But the jolly spirit of festivity had dissipated.

Down in the stables that night, Harry took extra-good care of Snowman. He vowed to himself that he would never, ever push his old horse too hard, this animal who had already brought his family untold blessings. Harry gave the horse a scratch on the withers. The old teddy bear rewarded him with a smile. They were survivors. Both of them.

On the ride back to Long Island, the front seat, as always, was littered with the prizes Snowman had won. There was the blue from the first fault-and-out class, and a few more reds and yellows. In his third year out, Snowman had not brought home the grand prize, but Harry cheered up the children by promising hamburgers for everyone.

Our horse is already a champion, he said. Nobody can take that away from him. And better yet, he's on his way home.

CHAPTER 27

NEW HOLLANDIA FARMS

ST. JAMES, LONG ISLAND, 1960-1969

Driving down Moriches Road on the way to the Knox School every day, Harry passed the old Butler place. It was a rambling dairy farm, more than forty acres, with a big barn and plenty of pasture. Overlooking the green fields stood a rambling white farmhouse with green shutters and lots of bedrooms. It was the kind of home you couldn't help daydreaming about living in. The kind of home that looked perfect for raising a big family.

Countless times, driving down that road, Harry had pointed to the property and said to Johanna that someday the farm would belong to them. The farm made its own cream and butter, and its rich ice cream was a popular local favorite in the summer. But the owner had died a couple of years earlier and the farm was no longer a moneymaking business.

It was ideal for the de Leyer family—just a mile up the road from Knox, with plenty of room for a large stable and even a place to build the big indoor ring Harry had always wanted. There would be plenty of room for their horses and growing family, and a big pasture for Snowman to walk around in, just a short distance from the beach.

Snowman's fame had brought plenty of business to Harry. His riding establishment was thriving. Sure, the Butler farm was run-down and its cattle barns would need to be converted, but Harry and Johanna had never been afraid of hard work. Once and for all, they decided to buy this farm. All up and down Moriches Road, little cookie-cutter houses were springing up, part of the postwar building boom. The de Leyers felt their new home on the dairy farm would be different. Something special.

After years of toil, the de Leyer family was living the dream Harry and Johanna had carried with them from Holland, along with their crate and meager savings: a good-sized piece of ground that belonged to them. Once again, they christened the farm Hollandia.

Though he had continued to show, winning ribbons in 1961 and 1962, Snowman was entered in fewer competitions these days. Harry had decided that the horse had done enough.

Here, on Hollandia Farms, in the grassy pasture under the pine trees, Snowman would live out his days. It took a lot of work to convert the old cattle barns into proper stables, but when it was finished, the Cinderella horse was given a place of honor, right near the barn's entrance.

And just because Snowy was showing less didn't mean he was forgotten. That fall, two children's books were published about Harry and his famous horse, one a picture book and the other for older readers. Harry toured Snowman all around the country to give exhibitions and do "signings." Harriet and Chef were enlisted as Harry's assistants, often holding Lady Gray when Snowman leapt over her, repeating his best-known trick. After the exhibitions, the brother and sister would varnish Snowman's hooves with hoof oil and sell his hoofprint "autograph" at twenty-five cents a pop. And soon enough, they got used to finding fan letters in their mailbox, addressed to Snowman.

One day, Harry took Snowman down to the bookstore in the small neighboring town of Stony Brook. Harry autographed the books, and the visiting children got to pet the horse and pluck a single strand from his mane. Even the Knox School girls had formed a fan club. Each girl got a signed book and a copy of the club membership certificate. Snowman still carried the timid girls around for lessons now and then, but as he got older, he spent most of his time just resting at home.

The day the brand-new horse arena at Hollandia was finished, the de Leyers threw a big party. All the neighbors were invited. The Knox girls and the other riding students were, too. There was a long, blue satin ribbon tied across a large entryway. Somebody had the idea that Snowman should be the first to enter the new arena. One of the kids ran to get a bridle and saddle, and Harry swung aboard, cantering toward the ribbon, planning to let Snowman break through. But at the last minute, the horse gathered up his knees and soared—clearing the ribbon by at least a foot. Everyone at the party clapped and cheered at the sight of the sweet old horse flying through the air.

Snowman had the run of the pasture. Best of all, he liked to go and stand under the pine trees down in the corner. He was always eager to carry one, two, or three of the kids around, and happy to head to the beach for a swim. Sometimes, Harry still let one of the children take the horse over a big jump. Harry and Johanna had come to expect that local children would

come around and ask after him. The books were always popular at the local library, and Snowman kept on winning new sets
of younger fans.

It was a good life for a horse, a life he'd earned.

In 1969, Harry got a phone call from Snowman's old friend
Marie Lafrenz. She was now chief publicist for the National
Horse Show, and she had an idea. The National Horse Show
had moved into the new Madison Square Garden. It was now
a modern sports arena, with big stadium seats. The huge new
stadium was more fit for basketball or hockey games than horse
shows. Besides, the times they were a-changing, and this kind
of spectacle, with women in evening gowns and men in top
hats, in what was now the Woodstock era, had lost its appeal.

Marie Lafrenz's main job was to see that the maximum
number of tickets got sold. Without box office, the National
Horse Show might not survive.

Marie knew just the draw to bring in loyal fans: invite one of
the most beloved horses in Garden history. So she asked Harry:
Would you like to officially retire Snowman in the Garden?

By now, Snowman had already been off the circuit for half
a decade. But Harry knew that his horse always enjoyed the
spectacle and the crowds. So he agreed. Yes, they would go to
the Garden to show Snowy one last time. The whole de Leyer
clan joined. Chef and Marty were so tall now that they towered
over their father, and Harriet had turned into a lovely young
lady. And another little girl, Anna-Marie, had been born into
the growing family. The girls and Johanna wore dresses, and the
boys were handsome in jackets and ties. Harry looked proud in

his riding clothes—an elegant navy blue hunt coat and white breeches.

At the Garden, Snowman wore his bridle one last time. The big white gates swung open and Harry de Leyer walked into the arena under blazing stadium lights. All cleaned up for the occasion, Snowman followed behind. Next came Johanna and the children. The lights were dimmed and the horse's coat gleamed under the spotlights. Music played over the giant loudspeakers, and men and women wearing evening finery came out, bearing a red-and-white blanket of roses. Folded up in their arms was a horse blanket in Hollandia's colors, green and yellow.

Snowman and Harry circled the spotlit arena. The roar of the crowd thundered through the giant hall as though it would last forever. The lights flashed on, then dimmed, then came up bright. The crowd kept clapping and cheering as they rose to a standing ovation.

As Harry walked around the ring, leading his beloved horse, he remembered every step that had brought them to this moment.

Snowman arriving at the chicken farm, his haunches covered in snow.

Finding the horse inside the paddock after he'd run away from the doctor's house.

His first few stumbling tries over the cavaletti poles.

And, of course, the moment when he won the national championship in '58.

But the strongest image was from that first moment on the slaughter truck, when something in the horse's expression had caught his eye. Harry couldn't help blinking back a tear on this night. He himself had almost missed this horse's gift. But somehow, the horse had always given him another chance. On the side of Snowman's cooler, in bold yellow letters, was his nickname: THE CINDERELLA HORSE.

On the way out of the Garden, the paparazzi waited to catch a glimpse of the equine celebrity. Flashbulbs popped and the big gray champion was caught for the last time—his picture was splashed huge across the back page of the *New York Post* under the headline SNOWMAN RETIRES. The New York hero had given his last performance.

CHAPTER 28

THE LEGACY OF A CHAMPION

ST. JAMES, LONG ISLAND

Snowman passed away on Harry and Johanna's farm in 1974. He stayed with his family to the last. Friendly visitors often came to visit him on the farm, wanting to see the eighty-dollar champion up close. When he had grown old and retired, Snowman liked to stand in the shade of the trees on the north end of the pasture, flicking his tail lazily, and perhaps remembering the days of his glory.

Snowman's story has never been forgotten. The tale of the rejected plow horse who became a champion has been told and retold, and the animal who almost ended up in a slaughterhouse has become one of history's best-loved horses.

If you want to visit Snowman's gravestone in New York, it still lies in the big field under the pine trees where the horse liked to stand, next to the fence along Moriches Road that leads down toward the beach. From time to time, people still come and knock on the farmhouse door to ask if they can see it.

The big gray is long gone, but living on is the memory of

the horse who was yoked to a plow, yet wanted to soar. Snow-man and Harry showed the world how extraordinary the most ordinary among us can be. Never give up, even when the ob-stacles seem sky-high. There is something extraordinary in all of us.

ACKNOWLEDGMENTS

To retell the story of *The Eighty-Dollar Champion*, I depended on the time, insights, and generosity of a great many people. First and foremost, this book could never have been written without the kindness and support of Harry and Joan de Leyer. They welcomed me and my family to their beautiful Nederland Farms in Virginia and shared their memories, photographs, and hospitality on countless occasions. Getting to know them was the greatest gift I can imagine.

I owe great thanks to my incomparable editor, Susanna Porter, who was passionate, insightful, and unflagging in her dedication, and to her assistant, Priyanka Krishnan, who helped me through the complicated task of putting a book together with patience and good grace. I am also deeply grateful to the entire incredible team at Ballantine who worked on the adult edition: Libby McGuire and Kim Hovey in the publisher's office, Benjamin Dreyer, Steve Messina, and Mark Maguire in managing editorial and production; cover designers Paolo Pepe and Victoria Allen; book designer Virginia Norey; Quinne Rogers and Kristin Fassler in marketing; and Cindy Murray and Susan Corcoran in publicity. Many thanks for the terrific work of the entire sales team in Westminster, Maryland, especially Cheryl Kelly, whose deep affection for this story was evident. I could not have asked for a more enthusiastic, hardworking, or talented group of people to have on my side.

I am extremely indebted to Jeff Kleinman at Folio Literary Management, whose absolute dedication, creativity, and belief in Snowman's story were instrumental every step of the way. I also want to thank Edith "Pete" Verloop and Corinne Kleinman for their love of horses and excellent hospitality, and for sharing their family history of life in wartime Holland.

Thanks to the National Sporting Library in Middleburg, Virginia, which awarded me a John H. Daniels Fellowship to support the writing of this book and gave me access to the library's superb equestrian collection. I'd especially like to thank Liz Tobey and Lisa Campbell for their help. Thanks also to Kathy Ball of the Smithtown Library for sharing the rich resources of its local history room, and George Allison of the Knox School for giving me access to the school and grounds, as well as delighting me with his wealth of knowledge about the institution and its history. I also appreciated Lucinda Dyer's incredible hard work and passionate love for big gray horses.

I relied on many people to share their insights with me, especially Bonnie Cornelius Spitzmiller, Phebe Phillips Byrne, Wendy Thomas, Harriet de Leyer, Bernie Traurig, Frank Guadagno, David Elliott, Marie Debany, Chris Hickey, Sarah Hochsteder, Kathy Kusner, and Kathleen Fallon. Thanks to Noelle King and Diane de Franceaux Grod for their terrific work in bringing the horse community together online. Thanks to William Zinsser for sharing his description of writing for the *New York Herald Tribune*.

Thanks Tasha Alexander, Jon Clinch, Melanie Benjamin, and Betsy Wilmerding for unflagging help and support.

Thanks to Ginger Letts for getting up at five A.M., hitching up the trailer, reminding me to remember my boots and britches, and driving me to horse shows, and also for telling me countless stories about life in an all-girls boarding school in the 1950s. I am indebted to Nora Alalou for her artistic acumen and cheerful unpaid tech support.

Great gratitude to Joey, Nora, Hannah, Willis, and Ali for being the most supportive, enthusiastic, fun, creative, and funny family a writer could ever have.

Last, I'd like to thank my own two-legged teachers, Donna Naylor, Pam Nelson, Hilda Gurney, Rob Gage, and Judy Martin, and my four-legged teachers, Foxy, Jack, Kim, Fuzzy, Princess, Norman, Mary, Ned, Boy, and Conrad Russell. Thanks to them, I know what it feels like to fly.

A CONVERSATION BETWEEN
ELIZABETH LETTS
AND HARRY DE LEYER

ELIZABETH LETTS: Harry, do you think living through the war and Nazi occupation taught you important life lessons? What were they?

HARRY DE LEYER: Most definitely, living through the war taught me very important lessons that have helped me throughout my life. The first is this: do not be afraid to make decisions. When you live through tough times, you have to act quickly, and you must have confidence in yourself and believe that you are making the right choice. I learned this skill when facing danger and hardship during the war, but it is something that I have carried with me throughout my life. Buying Snowman was a split-second decision, but somehow, I knew it was the right one.

The second and equally important lesson is this: do not be afraid of hard work. No problem is too great to overcome if you are willing to get up in the morning every single day ready to do your best. It's surprising how many difficulties can be overcome just by putting on your boots and working as hard as you can every single day.

EL: What surprised you most about life in the United States?

HDL: The language! When I arrived in Hoboken, I had a terrible time trying to find my way around. I couldn't figure out where to go or where to catch the train that would take me to my new job in North Carolina. I thought I knew a little bit of English, but I didn't understand what people were saying. Then, when I got to North Carolina, it seemed as if people were speaking an entirely different language, and I couldn't understand them, either. I did not realize that it would be such a challenge to figure out how to speak to people in English and understand what they were saying. When I first started teaching, I was very shy, always worried that I might say the wrong thing.

EL: Do you think your life would have turned out differently if you had walked away from Snowman that day?

HDL: Absolutely. Snowman put me on the top. I had only been in this country for a few years and nobody knew me. I did not make myself famous—Snowman did that. I don't think my life would have been the same if I hadn't found Snowman. That day, I thought I was unlucky, because of the snow and my flat tire, but looking back, it was the luckiest day of my life.

EL: Do you think the Snowman story could happen again?

HDL: In some ways, the world is a much different place today than it was when I was champion with Snowman, but in some ways, I don't think it has changed that much. It takes the same skills to get to the top today that were needed fifty years ago: a little bit of luck, a lot of determination, and most of all, a belief that you can do it. Horses are just like people: each one has some hidden potential. What it takes to bring out the best in a horse, or in anyone, is to believe in him one hundred percent. You don't have to "make" the horse. The good Lord made the horse. All you have to do is go along with him and find out what he is good at, and the rest will take care of itself. Champions are not necessarily the best, or the most beautiful, or the most expensive; champions are the ones with the biggest dreams and the heart to make those dreams come true.

EL: What has it been like for you to see the story of you and your horse become so well known more than fifty years after you first won the championship at Madison Square Garden?

HDL: One of the biggest honors for me was to be invited to the Washington International Horse Show to present the President's Cup [a trophy that was donated to the horse show by John F. Kennedy and was first presented in 1961 by Jackie Kennedy]. I still remember how proud I was the day that I rode Snowman in front of the presidential box at this prestigious horse show. For an immigrant like me, it was an enormous honor. But I never dreamed that in 2011, on the fiftieth anniversary of the President's Cup competition, I would be invited into the arena to present the trophy to the winner. That was a feeling that I will never forget.

EL: These are difficult economic times. What would you tell today's generations about how to succeed when they face adversity?

HDL: What I would tell young people is that if you work hard and believe in yourself you can make your own luck. When I went through Ellis Island and landed in Hoboken, I wasn't sure what the future held, but I knew that I was willing to do what I needed to get ahead. I did not expect to be able to work with horses, but just by doing what I loved, I was able to find a way to succeed and work in a job that I loved. But for young people just starting out, it's important to remember that there is a lot of hard work doing things that are not very glamorous or interesting before you ever get near a spotlight. Still, if you do each task right, every day, even the humble jobs, you will make steady progress toward your goals. When times are tough, it's easy to get discouraged, but if you imagine what you want and keep going after it, you will be amazed at what you can achieve.

EL: Do you have a favorite memory of Snowman?

HDL: I have so many favorite memories of Snowman that it is hard to choose just one, but I'd have to say that my favorite was to see Snowman swimming with all of my children on his back, holding his nose up out of the water and having such a good time. It was a wonderful feeling to see them all enjoying themselves and to know that the horse was taking care of them. Of all of the wonderful moments, I think that was the most wonderful of all.

EL: Are any of your children still involved with horses?

HDL: Oh, yes indeed. Several of my children grew up to be very skilled riders and horse trainers, following in the de Leyer tradition. Now there are even de Leyer grandchildren competing in the show ring just as I did.

A CONVERSATION WITH
THE AUTHOR

QUESTION: Elizabeth, what drew you to this story?

ELIZABETH LETTS: There is a special magic that happens in a horse story. From the first time I saw a picture of Harry and Snowman, I knew that these two shared a special bond and that somehow, together, they were greater than the sum of their parts. I hoped, through this story, to bring that magic to life for my readers.

Q: Do you see any parallels between the late 1950s, when the story was set, and the times we live in now?

EL: It's easy to look back at the late 1950s with a sense of nostalgia, and we remember them as "happy days." But the story of Snowman and Harry reminds us vividly that, in fact, it was a time of rapid and dramatic transition, with new media replacing old, and the global realities of the atomic age putting people on edge. Harry was one of millions of people who were displaced by World War II and had to start over from scratch. The job skills he brought to this country, as a farmer and a horseman, were not the kind of training that would make it easy for him to make a living. And yet, somehow, his fundamental qualities of character, as well as his belief in a better future, were enough to give him a start. We would all do well to look to his example as a way to work toward a better future.

Q: After researching the history of the condition of the horse in the mid-twentieth century, do you think life for horses is better now or worse than it was fifty years ago?

EL: That is a complicated question. In some ways, life is better, as there have been improvements in humane treatment of horses that are used for sport. But in other ways, the life of horses right now is particularly difficult. During rough economic times, animals are often hard hit when their cash-strapped owners are no longer able to care for them. Horses are perhaps the most affected: keeping horses is expensive and labor intensive, and they are often considered a luxury. When people start abandoning their horses, it leads to more neglected horses needing love, care, and good homes.

Q: If people are concerned with horse welfare, what can they do to get involved?

EL: There are so many ways to get involved with helping horses. You can volunteer for a horse rescue organization, or get involved in a group that retrains horses for second lives, for example, therapeutic riding. You do not have to have a lot of money to be able to do something to make the lives of horses better. A reliable list of organizations involved in horse welfare can be found at the American Horse Council (horsecouncil.org).

Q: What was the most rewarding thing for you about writing the story of Harry and Snowman?

EL: For me, the most rewarding thing has been to meet people who remember hearing the story of Snowman as children, and how the incredible tale of the young immigrant and his unlikely plow horse–turned–champion was an inspiration in their lives. As I've gone around the country talking to people about this story, I've been approached countless times by fans with decades-old memories, some clutching faded photographs of Snowman, or stories of the ways that Snowman's story inspired them—to become veterinarians, or to volunteer for animal welfare, or to overcome some terrible problem or adversity to get closer to a seemingly impossible dream. It is my great hope that a new generation of readers will discover this magical story and go on to pursue great goals of their own.

BIBLIOGRAPHY

"Advertising: Man in a Hurry." *Time*, Mar. 6, 1950.

"Alice Higgins, Magazine Writer on Equestrian Sports, Is Dead." *New York Times*, Sept. 19, 1974.

Ames, Lynne. "At Work: Where Do the Amish Train Their Horses?" *New York Times*, Oct. 18, 2003.

"And a Bow to the Supporting Cast." *Sports Illustrated*, Jan. 5, 1959.

Aurandt, Paul. "Snow Man." In *Paul Harvey's The Rest of the Story*. Edited and compiled by Lynne Harvey. New York: Doubleday, 1977.

Aurichio, Andrea. "And Thereby Hang Some Tails." *New York Times*, July 20, 1980.

Austin, Dale. "Snowman Wins Jump-off in Show, Two Mounts Unseat Riders, Hurdles Fall." *Washington Post*, Oct. 28, 1960.

Baker, E. T. *The Home Veterinarian's Handbook: A Guide for Handling Emergencies in Farm Animals and Poultry*. New York: Macmillan, 1944.

"Black Atom Takes Horse Show Lead." *Washington Post*, Oct. 26, 1960.

Bracker, Milton. "Philadelphia Society, Changing but Changeless." *New York Times*, Jan. 14, 1957.

Brewer, Toni. "Washington International." *Chronicle of the Horse*, Oct. 24, 1958.

Bryan, Bill. "History of the United States Equestrian Team." *Chronicle of the Horse*, Oct. 31, 1958.

Bryan, Bill. "U.S. Team Success." *Chronicle of the Horse*, Aug. 15, 1958.

"Business." *Time*, Dec. 30, 1957.

"By Way of Report: John Huston's Full Slate—La Dolce Vita Is Acquired—Snowman Saga." *New York Times*, Jan. 22, 1961.

"Chapot, U.S., Wins Jump-off in Show; Beats Germany's Winkler by 1 Second—President Sees Washington Event." *New York Times*, Oct. 16, 1958.

"Children's Services." *Chronicle of the Horse*, June 12, 1959.

Christmas, Anne. "Washington International." *Chronicle of the Horse*, Nov. 18, 1960.

"Classy Jumpers to Battle at Ox Ridge." *Sunday Bridgeport Herald*, May 29, 1960.

"Conversation Piece." *Chronicle of the Horse*, Aug. 29, 1958.

Corrigan, Ed. "De Leyer's Two Jumpers Help Argentines over Rough Spot." *New York Times*, Nov. 28, 1971.

Corrigan, Ed. "Doomed Horse Leaps from Kill Pen to Fame." *Chicago Tribune*, Nov. 8, 1958.

Corrigan, Ed. "Serious Fall off Horse Fails to Deter Youngster." *New York Times*, Dec. 11, 1977.

Corrigan, Ed. "Snowman Returns for Final Accolade." *New York Times*, Nov. 9, 1969.

Corry, John. "Showing Horses on a Shoestring: Many Exhibitors Do Own Stable Work to Save Money." *New York Times*, Nov. 11, 1958.

Crago, Judy. "Selection, Training, and Care." In *The Complete Book of Show Jumping*, edited by William Steinkraus and Michael Clayton. New York: Crown, 1975.

"Crowd in Furs Sees Piping Rock Horse Show." *New York Times*, Oct. 7, 1909.

"Dappled Gray Scores, Snowman Gets Meyner Prize at Paramus Horse Show." *New York Times*, Oct. 13, 1958.

De Butts, Mary Custis Lee, and Rosalie Noland Woodland, eds. *Charlotte Haxall Noland, 1883–1969*. Middleburg, VA: Foxcroft, 1971.

"De Leyer, Maker of Champions, Dreams of His Greatest One." *New York Times*, Mar. 7, 1965.

"De Leyer Paces Show." *New York Times*, July 21, 1958.

Devereux, Frederick L. *Famous American Horses: 21 Steeplechasers, Trotters, Cow-ponies, Flat Racers, Show Horses and Battle Mounts That Have Made History*. Old Greenwich, CT: Devin-Adair, 1975.

"Devon." *Chronicle of the Horse*, June 14, 1958.

"Diamant Captures 3d Jump-off, Wins Horse Show Prize." *New York Times*, Sept. 12, 1958.

"Diamant Registers Horse Show Victory." *New York Times*, Sept. 16, 1958.

Dioguardi, Ralph. "The Horse Nobody Wanted." *Smithtown Sunday Digest*, May 20, 1979.

"Douglaston Wins Horse Show Title." *New York Times*, May 5, 1958.

Edwards, Russell. "National Horse Show—Good-by to the Garden." *New York Times*, Oct. 8, 1967.

Edwards, Russell. "National Horse Show Here Has a 76-Year History of Strange and Wondrous Things." *New York Times*, Nov. 1, 1958.

"$80 Wonder Horse Worth $25,000: Snowman, the Equine Phenomenon, Stars at Children's Services Horse Show, May 15–17." *Hartford Courant*, May 10, 1959.

"Equestrian Team Will Be Assisted at Fete in Darien." *New York Times*, June 11, 1961.

"Fairfield County Hunt." *Chronicle of the Horse*, July 11, 1958.

"FBI Rangers View G.I. Horse Trading." *New York Times*, May 14, 1946.

Fitzgerald, F. Scott. *The Great Gatsby*. 1925. Reprint, New York: Scribner, 1999.

"Five Cubans Stage Protest of Countrymen in Show." *New York Times*, Nov. 5, 1958.

Fleming, Geoffrey. *Images of America: St. James*. Charleston, SC: Arcadia Publishing, 2002.

"Fly Your Bloodstock." Advertisement. *Chronicle of the Horse*, Oct. 31, 1958.

Forgeron, Harry V. "Town Puts Heart in Its Horse Show: Port Washington Lions Find Willing Hands for Event That Built Ballfield." *New York Times*, May 15, 1960.

Franck, Peggy Miller. *Prides Crossing: The Unbridled Life and Impatient Times of Eleo Sears*. Beverly, MA: Commonwealth Editions, 2009.

Fussell, Paul. *Class: A Guide Through the American Status System*. New York: Touchstone, 1992.

Gava, Adrienne E. *Dark Horse: A Life of Anna Sewell*. Thrupp, UK: Sutton, 2004.

"Gayford, Canada, First in Jumping." *New York Times*, Nov. 4, 1960.

"Genuine Risk Dies; Filly Won Kentucky Derby." *New York Times*, Aug. 18, 2008.

"German Rider Clinches Laurels in Washington Show." *New York Times*, Oct. 15, 1958.

Gish, Noel J. *Looking Back Through the Lens*. Smithtown, NY: Smithtown Historical Society, 1996.

Goldstein, Andrew. "Joe Goldstein, Dogged New York Sports Promoter, Dies at 81." *New York Times*, Feb. 15, 2009.

Gould, John. "Hoss Trading: A Lesson for Diplomats." *New York Times Magazine*, Nov. 16, 1947.

Green, Ben K. *Horse Tradin'*. New York: Alfred A. Knopf, 1963.

"Green Is Injured in Horse Show Test." *New York Times*, Sept. 16, 1955.

Greene, Ann Norton. *Horses at Work: Harnessing Power in Industrial America*. Cambridge, MA: Harvard University Press, 2008.

"Grim Reaper at National." *Chronicle of the Horse*, Nov. 21, 1958.

Halberstam, David. *The Fifties*. New York: Random House, 1993.

"Harold S. Vanderbilt and Miss Sears." *New York Times*, Aug. 23, 1911.

Harris, Bradley. "The Early Beginnings of the Smithtown Hunt." *Smithtown News*, July 31, 2008.

Harris, Bradley. "Growing Up on the La Rosa Estate in Nissequogue." *Smithtown News*, Sept. 18, 2008.

Harris, Bradley. "James Clinch Smith Brings Polo to Smithtown." *Smithtown News*, Dec. 4, 2008.

Harris, Bradley. "The Knox School Finds a Home in Nissequogue." *Smithtown News*, Sept. 25, 2008.

Harris, Bradley. "Lathrop Brown Estate, a Southern Colonial Mansion." *Smithtown News*, Aug. 28, 2008.

Harris, Bradley. "Ponies Once Pranced at St. James Driving Park." *Smithtown News*, Nov. 27, 2008.

Harris, Bradley. "The Smithtown Horse Show." *Smithtown News*, Jan. 8, 2009.

Harris, Bradley. "The Smithtown Polo Club." *Smithtown News*, Jan. 1, 2009.

Harris, Bradley. "Snowman, the Cinderella Horse of Hollandia Farms." *Smithtown News*, July 10, 2008.

Harris, Bradley. "Still Tracking Foxes in the Smithtown Hunt." *Smithtown News*, Aug. 21, 2008.

Higgins, Alice. "Deutschland über Alles: At Brand-New Washington Show, Germans Collected Everything but the Tickets." *Sports Illustrated*, Oct. 27, 1958.

Higgins, Alice. "Exit Jumping: Andante, an Aged Prima Donna, Begins Her Last Season with a Flamboyant Win at Devon." *Sports Illustrated*, June 20, 1960.

Higgins, Alice. "German Cliffhanger." *Sports Illustrated*, Nov. 24, 1958.

Higgins, Alice. "Revival of an Old Ruckus." *Sports Illustrated*, Nov. 14, 1960.

Higgins, Alice. "The 67th National Horse Show Had Some Great Horses, Some Thrilling Riders, and Some Unexpected Light Moments." *Sports Illustrated*, Nov. 21, 1955.

Higgins, Alice. "Thinker on Horseback." *Sports Illustrated*, Dec. 15, 1958.

Higgins, Alice. "The Year of the Jumpers: A Spectacular Open Event in New York Tops a Season of Excellent Performances Around the Country by American and Foreign Horses." *Sports Illustrated*, Nov. 20, 1961.

Higginson, A. Henry, and Julian Ingersoll Chamberlain. *The Hunts of the United States and Canada: Their Masters, Hounds and Histories*. Boston: Frank L. Wiles, 1908.

Hopper, Hedda. "Hollywood." *Hartford Courant*, Nov. 17, 1960.

"Horse Saved from Execution Becomes Champion." *Bridgeport Day*, Nov. 7, 1958.

"Horses for Sale at Auction." *Horse Magazine*, April 1956.

"Horse Show Begins, U.S. Riders Featured." *Spokesman-Review*, Nov. 1, 1959.

"Horse Show Ends with Many Fetes." *New York Times*, Nov. 13, 1957.

"Horse Showing Is a Grim Business." *Palm Beach Post*, Nov. 17, 1962.

"Horse-Show Jumping Taken by Uncle Max." *New York Times*, Oct. 21, 1962.

"Horses to Be Improved; Federal Authorities, Through Remount Program, to Aid Breeders." *New York Times*, June 8, 1919.

"Horse That Jumps: From the Slaughterhouse to the Motion Picture Screen." *Fitchburg Sentinel*, Dec. 30, 1959.

Hunter, Jane. *How Young Ladies Became Girls.* New Haven, CT: Yale University Press, 2003.

"Hunter Tests Led by Paxson Entry." *New York Times*, June 14, 1959.

Igou, Brad. "An Amishman Talks About Horses." *Amish Country News*, Winter 1996.

"In the Country." *Chronicle of the Horse*, Dec. 1, 1959.

"Jumper Windsor Castle Is Sold in $50,000 Deal." *New York Times*, Nov. 6, 1959.

"Jumping King Snow Man Is Hurt in Fall." *Chicago Daily Tribune*, June 26, 1960.

"Junk Wagon Horse Takes a Fling at Broadway Chase." *New York Times*, Apr. 17, 1956.

Kluger, Richard. *The Paper: The Life and Death of the "New York Herald Tribune."* New York: Alfred A. Knopf, 1986.

Kunhardt, Philip B. "The Farm Horse That Became a Champion." *Animals You Will Never Forget.* Pleasantville, NY: Reader's Digest Books, 1969.

Lafrenz, Marie C. "Horse Show Publicity." *Whole Horse Catalogue.* Edited by Steven D. Price. New York: Fireside, 1998.

Lafrenz, Marie C. "Increase in Number of Thoroughbreds." *New York Herald Tribune*, Mar. 6, 1960.

Lafrenz, Marie C. "Professional Versus Amateur." *New York Herald Tribune*, Apr. 19, 1960.

"Lakeville." *Chronicle of the Horse*, Aug. 15, 1958.

Langdon, John. *Horses, Oxen, and Technological Innovation.* Cambridge: Cambridge University Press, 1986.

Leerhson, Charles. *Crazy Good: The True Story of Dan Patch, the Most Famous Horse in America.* New York: Simon & Schuster, 2009.

Lipsyte, Robert. "Joey Goldstein." Sports of the Times. *New York Times*, Mar. 18, 1969.

Littauer, Mary Aiken. "Whither Horse Shows." *Chronicle of the Horse*, Sept. 19, 1958.

Littauer, Vladimir S. *Common Sense Horsemanship.* New York: Van Nostrand, 1951.

Littauer, Vladimir S. *Jumping the Horse.* New York: Derrydale, 1931.

Livingston, Phil, and Ed Roberts. *War Horse: Mounting the Cavalry with America's Finest Horses*. Albany, TX: Bright Sky Press, 2003.

"Local Riders and Mounts Take Part in International Show." *Long Islander*, Nov. 14, 1958.

Longrigg, Roger. *The Complete History of Fox Hunting*. New York: Clarkson Potter, 1975.

Lucey, Virginia. "Afternoon Events Halted by Rain." *Hartford Courant*, Sept. 28, 1958.

Lucey, Virginia. "Benefit Horse Show Opens with Jumpers." *Hartford Courant*, May 16, 1959.

Lucey, Virginia. "Saddle and Spur." *Hartford Courant*, Oct. 5, 1958.

Lucey, Virginia. "Saddle and Spur." *Hartford Courant*, Nov. 16, 1958.

Lucey, Virginia. "Saddle and Spur." *Hartford Courant*, Sept. 6, 1959.

Lucey, Virginia. "Saddle and Spur." *Hartford Courant*, Nov. 1, 1959.

Lucey, Virginia. "Saddle and Spur." *Hartford Courant*, Nov. 11, 1959.

Lucey, Virginia. "Saddle and Spur." *Hartford Courant*, Nov. 22, 1959.

Lucey, Virginia. "Saddle and Spur." *Hartford Courant*, July 24, 1960.

Lucey, Virginia. "Two Jumpers Capture Honors at Horse Show." *Hartford Courant*, May 18, 1959.

Lyon, Robert. *On Any Given Sunday: A Life of Bert Bell*. Philadelphia: Temple University Press, 2010.

Mancuso, Lisa. "Thrill of the Hunt: Equestrian Honored with Club Lifetime Award." *Smithtown News*, Apr. 1, 2010.

"Mann Horses Pace Show." *New York Times*, Sept. 5, 1957.

McCardle, Dorothy. "Jumping Horse Cops Fame, Wealth." *Washington Post*, Sept. 18, 1960.

McGowan, Dean. "Pat Smythe, Ace Woman Rider, Takes U.S. Officials over Jumps." *New York Times*, Nov. 5, 1957.

McGowan, Dean. "Steinkraus Scores for Third U.S. Jumping Triumph at National Horse Show." *New York Times*, Nov. 7, 1958.

McGowan, Dean. "West Germany's Thiedemann Scores Twice at Garden." *New York Times*, Nov. 11, 1958.

"McLain Street Wins Open Jumper Title." *New York Times*, Sept. 10, 1961.

McShane, Clay, and Joel A. Tarr. *The Horse in the City: Living Machines in the Nineteenth Century*. Baltimore: Johns Hopkins University Press, 2007.

Meagher, Thomas. *The Gigantic Book of Horse Wisdom*. New York: Skyhorse, 2007.

"Mickey Walsh, Horse Trainer, 86." *New York Times*, Aug. 19, 1983.

Mischka, Joseph. *The Percheron Horse in America*. Whitewater, WI: Heart Prairie Press, 1991.

"Miss Lida Fleitmann, Horsewoman, to Wed." *New York Times*, Feb. 1, 1922.

"Miss Maloney Guides Kitalpha to Pony Crown at Southampton." *New York Times*, Aug. 19, 1962.

"Miss Payne Rides Mare to 4 Blues." *New York Times*, June 22, 1958.

"Miss Sears Guest of Mrs. Belmont." *New York Times*, Aug. 14, 1911.

"Miss Sears Not Engaged; Member of Her Family Denies She Is Betrothed to Harold S. Vanderbilt." *New York Times*, Aug. 11, 1911.

"Miss Sears' Skating Outfit; She Prefers Cap and Muff of Knitted Wool for Cold Days." *New York Times*, Feb. 19, 1912.

"Miss Sears Turns Runaway, Swerves Animal from Bolting Among Spectators at Lawn Tennis Match." *New York Times*, Sept. 28, 1911.

Montgomery, Rutherford. *Snowman*. New York: Duell, Sloan, and Pearce, 1962.

Moore, Major-General Sir John. *Our Servant the Horse: An Appreciation of the Part Played by Animals During the War, 1914–1918*. London: H & W Brown, 1931.

"More Children Saddle Up Each Year Despite Cost." *New York Times*, Nov. 5, 1957.

Morenstern, George. "Minding My Own Business: Let Us Now Praise Famous Horses." *Chicago Tribune*, June 17, 1973.

"National Horse Show." *Chronicle of the Horse*, Nov. 21, 1958.

"National Horse Show Begins Run." *Schenectady Gazette*, Nov. 4, 1958.

"National's Diamond Jubilee." *Chronicle of the Horse*, Sept. 12, 1958.

"Naute Mia Heads Working Hunters." *New York Times*, Sept. 7, 1958.

"New Country Club Piping Rock Will Be Devoted to Sports Chiefly with Horses." *New York Times*, Oct. 9, 1911.

"New Look at the Capitol Armory." *Lewiston Daily Sun,* Jan. 12, 1961.

"The 1958 PHA Trophy." Photograph with caption. *Chronicle of the Horse,* Oct. 10, 1958.

"Nosing Around." *St. James Times,* July 22, 1993.

"The Not-So-Grave Tale of the Cinderella Horse." *St. James Times-Beacon,* Mar. 14, 1991.

Obituary, Marie C. Lafrenz. *US Eventing News,* May 18, 2007.

O'Dea, Joseph. *DVM, Olympic Vet.* Geneseo, NY: Castlerea Press, 1996.

The Official Report of the Organizing Committee for the XIV Olympiad. London: Organizing Committee for the XIV Olympiad, 1948.

"Old Nag's Long Jump from Plow Horse; Discarded Farm Horse Finds Unexpected Fame," *Life,* Nov. 9, 1959.

"Open Jumping Goes to Windsor Castle." *New York Times,* Aug. 12, 1960.

Parker, Betsy Burke. "Living Legends: Harry De Leyer Riding into the Future in the Saddle of His Past." *In and Around Horse Country,* Feb.–Mar., 2009.

"Paxson's Gelding Takes Third Blue; Flying Curlew Sets Pace in Piping Rock Fixture; Snowman Triumphs." *New York Times,* Sept. 17, 1960.

"Peter Gunn Scores in Fairfield Show." *New York Times,* Jun. 25, 1961.

"Petersen Gelding Wins Hunter Prize." *New York Times,* Aug. 20, 1962.

"Petersen Horse Captures Trophy." *New York Times,* Aug. 7, 1960.

"Piping Rock Horse Show." Photograph with caption. *Chronicle of the Horse,* Oct. 3, 1958.

"Piping Rock's Millionaire's Colony Opens New Club." *New York Times,* May 26, 1912.

"Presentation of the 1958 PHA Award." Photograph with caption. *Chronicle of the Horse,* Nov. 21, 1958.

"Promissory Notes of the Past Screen Season." *New York Times,* Dec. 31, 1961.

Rendel, John. "8-Day Horse Show Opens Here Today; Jumping Teams Will Parade Around the Garden Ring in Formal Ceremony." *New York Times,* Nov. 5, 1957.

Rendel, John. "German Riders Score in Horse Show; 24-Fault Effort Wins Nations Cup." *New York Times,* 1958.

Rendel, John. "Irish Rider Takes a First and a Second as National Horse Show Opens Here." *New York Times*, Nov. 1, 1961.

Rendel, John. "Irish Team Wins Good Will Challenge Trophy in Horse Show at Garden." *New York Times*, Nov. 4, 1961.

Rendel, John. "Stumble Results in a Broken Neck." *New York Times*, Nov. 5, 1960.

Rendel, John. "United States Team Retires Special Challenge Trophy at Show in Garden." *New York Times*, Nov. 5, 1958.

Rendel, John. "Wiley Is Winner Second Straight Year." *New York Times*, Nov. 5, 1958.

Rodenas, Paula. *The de Nemethy Years: One Man's Influence on American Riding*. New York: Arco, 1983.

"Roy Campanella Continues to Gain; Injured Catcher Gets Some Feeling Back in Body, but Legs Still Paralyzed." *New York Times*, Jan. 31, 1958.

Rule Book. American Horse Shows Association, 1958.

Rust, Richard. *Renegade Champion: The Unlikely Rise of Fitzrada*. Lanham, MD: Taylor Trade, 2008.

Safire, William. "Locust Valley Lockjaw." On Language. *New York Times Magazine*, Jan. 18, 1987.

"Sands Point." *Chronicle of the Horse*, June 22, 1958.

Scanlan, Lawrence. *Secretariat: The Horse That God Built*. New York: Thomas Dunne Books, 2007.

Self, Margaret Cabell. *The Horseman's Encyclopedia*. New York: A. S. Barnes, 1946.

"Sidelights of the National." *Chronicle of the Horse*, Nov. 21, 1958.

"65th National Horse Show to Begin an Eight-Day Run at Garden on Tuesday." *New York Times*, Nov. 1, 1953.

Smith, Margaret L. "National Horse Show." *Chronicle of the Horse*, Nov. 21, 1958.

Smith, Margaret L. "Penna National Horse Show." *Chronicle of the Horse*, Nov. 7, 1958.

Smith, Margaret L. Scrapbooks. In the collection of the National Sporting Library, Middleburg, VA.

"Smithtown." *Chronicle of the Horse*, Sept. 12, 1958.

"Snowman and Pedro Capture Jumper Crowns in Connecticut." *New York Times*, June 27, 1960.

"Snowman Captures Horse Show Honors." *New York Times*, May 22, 1961.

"Snowman Featured in Benefit Next Week." *New York Observer*, June 16, 1963.

"Snowman First in Jumper Class, Windsor Castle Second in 1959 Ranking." *New York Times*, Jan. 3, 1960.

"Snow Man First in Jumping Event; Beats Diamant for Title in Piping Rock Horse Show." *New York Times*, Sept. 15, 1958.

"Snow Man Gains Jumper Laurels." *New York Times*, May 8, 1961.

"Snowman Gives Exhibition Today in Horse Show." *Washington Post*, Sept. 24, 1960.

"Snowman Has a Rival, and She's in His Own Stable." *Port Washington News*, Nov. 5, 1959.

"Snow Man Injured in Jump." *New York Times*, June 26, 1960.

"Snowman Leaves Memories in Hearts of Horsemen." *Smithtown Messenger*, Oct. 3, 1974.

"Snowman, Legendary Jumper, Retired to St. James Pasture." *Smithtown Messenger*, Nov. 20, 1969.

"Snow Man Scores in L.I. Horse Show." *New York Times*, June 9, 1958.

"Snowman Takes Jumper Honors; De Leyer's Gelding Defeats High Tore for Open Title in North Shore Show." *New York Times*, Sept. 13, 1959.

"Snowman Tops at Ox Ridge." *Bridgeport Post*, June 20, 1960.

"Snowman Triumphs in Second Jump-off." *New York Times*, June 24, 1960.

"Snowman Winning Honors in National Horse Show." *Smithtown Messenger*, Nov. 2, 1961.

"Society Aids at Piping Rock Club." *New York Times*, Oct. 5, 1912.

"Society Amateurs in the Saddle: Piping Rock Horse Show Attracts Hunting Set to Locust Valley Grounds." *New York Times*, Oct. 4, 1913.

"Society: She Ain't What She Used to Be." *Time*, Nov. 9, 1962.

"Sport: Back in the Saddle." *Time*, Nov. 13, 1950.

"Sport: Grand Old Girl." *Time*, Dec. 25, 1939.

"The Sporting Calendar." *Chronicle of the Horse*, Aug. 29, 1958.

Sprague, Kurth. *The National Horse Show: A Centennial History, 1883–1983*. New York: National Horse Show Foundation, 1983.

Steinkraus, William. *Great Horses of the United States Equestrian Team*. New York: Dodd, Mead & Company, 1977.

Steinkraus, William. *Riding and Jumping*. Garden City, NY: Doubleday, 1961.

"Steinkraus Captures Jumping Event: Course Cleared in 32.39 Seconds." *New York Times*, Nov. 10, 1969.

"Steinkraus Wins at London Show." *New York Times*, July 21, 1958.

Stoneridge, M. A. *A Horse of Your Own*. Garden City, NY: Doubleday, 1963.

Stoneridge, M. A., ed. "How to Evaluate a Horse for Soundness." In *Practical Horseman's Book of Horsekeeping*. New York: Doubleday, 1983.

Stott, Bill. "Anthem of 1950s America." billstott.blogspot.com/search /label/American%20cultural%20history.

Tantalo, Victor. "Horse Show Promotion." *Chronicle of the Horse*, May 8, 1959.

"Thomas School Team Champions at Knox School Horse Show." *Long Islander*, May 1, 1958.

"Three Blues Won by Mann Entries; Fiore Rides Riviera Wonder and Topper to Victories at Stony Brook Show." *New York Times*, Sept. 6, 1957.

"3 De Leyer Horses Win at Stony Brook." *New York Times*, Sept. 5, 1958.

"Towson Man Wins London Horse Show." *Washington Post*, July 24, 1958.

"U.S. Riders Take Second, Third in Irish Show." *Washington Post*, Aug. 6, 1958.

Van Liew, Barbara F., and Elizabeth Shepherd, eds. *Head of the Harbor: A Journey Through Time*. Laurel, NY: Main Road Books, 2005.

Vecsey, George. "Raceway Era: When Dog Days Became Trotter Nights." *New York Times*, July 22, 1988.

"Walsh's Girls Help Him over Belmont Hurdles; Trainer's Daughters Exercise Horses 6 Days a Week." *New York Times*, May 27, 1958.

Weiler, A. H. "Movie to Relate Story of a Horse; Bob Hope May Play Role of Snowman's Rescuer." *New York Times*, Sept. 25, 1961.

Weiler, A. H. "Promissory Notes of the Past Screen Season." *New York Times*, Dec. 31, 1961.

Weiner, Tim. "Robert Lantz, Agent to the Stars, Dies." *New York Times*, Oct. 20, 2007.

White, Claire Nicolas. "Cinderella Horse Stars on L.I." *New York Times*, Oct. 22, 1972.

"Wiley Is Winner Second Straight Year, U.S. Rider Takes West Point Trophy Again at Garden." *New York Times*, Nov. 5, 1958.

"Wiley Triumphs After Jump-off." *New York Times*, Nov. 8, 1959.

"Windsor Castle Takes Jumping Title at Armory." *Washington Post*, Oct. 31, 1960.

"Woman Rider Hurt in Jumping Contest." *New York Times*, Oct. 2, 1915.

Zinsser, William. "The Daily Miracle: Life with the Mavericks and Oddballs at the *Herald Tribune*." *American Scholar* 77, no. 1 (Winter 2008).

IMAGE CREDITS

PAGE II-III: Photograph by George Silk; Time-Life Pictures/Getty Images.

INSERT

PAGE 1: *Top:* courtesy of the personal collection of Harry de Leyer. *Bottom:* courtesy of the personal collection of Harry de Leyer.

PAGE 2: Courtesy of Bonnie Cornelius Spitzmiller from *Rose Leaves,* the Knox School yearbook, 1957. Used with the permission of the Knox School.

PAGE 3: *Top:* courtesy of Bonnie Cornelius Spitzmiller from *Rose Leaves,* the Knox School yearbook, 1957; used with the permission of the Knox School. *Bottom:* courtesy of Bonnie Cornelius Spitzmiller from *Rose Leaves,* the Knox School yearbook, 1957; used with the permission of the Knox School.

PAGE 4: *Top:* courtesy of the personal collection of Harry de Leyer; *Bottom:* courtesy of the personal collection of Harry de Leyer.

PAGE 5: *Top left:* photograph by Marshall Hawkins, courtesy of Robert McClanahan. *Top right:* photograph by George Silk; Time-Life Pictures/Getty Images; *Bottom:* courtesy of the personal collection of Harry de Leyer.

PAGES 6-7: Photograph by George Silk; Time-Life Pictures/Getty Images.

PAGE 8: *Top:* photograph by George Silk; Time-Life Pictures/Getty Images. *Bottom:* photograph by George Silk; Time-Life Pictures/Getty Images.

PAGE 9: *Top:* courtesy of the personal collection of Harry de Leyer. *Bottom:* courtesy of the personal collection of Harry de Leyer.

PAGE 10: *Top:* courtesy of the National Sporting Library & Museum Archives.

PAGE 11: *Top:* courtesy of the National Sporting Library & Museum Archives. *Bottom:* courtesy of the National Sporting Library & Museum Archives.

PAGE 12: *Top:* photograph by Stan Wayman; Time-Life Pictures/Getty Images. *Center:* photograph by Gjon Mili; Time-Life Pictures/Getty Images. *Bottom:* photograph by Stan Wayman; Time-Life Pictures/Getty Images.

PAGE 13: Cartoon by Willard Mullins, courtesy of Shirley Mullins Rhodes.

PAGE 14: *Top:* photograph by George Silk; Time-Life Pictures/Getty Images. *Bottom:* © Bill Ray.

PAGE 15: *Top:* courtesy of the personal collection of Harry de Leyer. *Bottom:* © Bill Ray.

PAGE 16: *Top:* courtesy of the personal collection of Harry de Leyer. *Bottom:* courtesy of the personal collection of Harry de Leyer.

INDEX

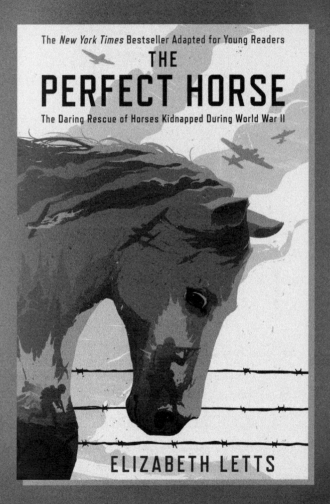

The *New York Times* Bestseller Adapted for Young Readers

THE
PERFECT HORSE

The Daring Rescue of Horses Kidnapped During World War II

ELIZABETH LETTS

ABOUT THE AUTHOR

ELIZABETH LETTS is the #1 *New York Times* bestselling author of *The Perfect Horse, The Eighty-Dollar Champion,* and *Finding Dorothy,* as well as two novels, *Quality of Care* and *Family Planning.* A competitive equestrian in her youth, Letts rode for California in the North American Junior and Young Rider Championships. She lives in Southern California.

elizabethletts.com